CHANGING ME

Becoming A
Woman Of Faith

DEBORAH CHAPMAN

CHANGING ME

LAYOUT & TYPEFACE

OpenOffice.org Writer, ver. 2.0.4 | www.openoffice.org

Berling Antiqua
COPYRIGHT 1990-2001 AGFA MONOTYPE CORPORATION. ALL RIGHTS RESERVED.
Berling Antiqua was designed by Swedish calligrapher and typographer Karl
Erik Forsberg and issued in 1951 by the Berlingska Stilgjuteriet foundry of Lund.
The design features of Berling lend itself to minimum interruption in the flow
of reading, making it an ideal choice for book setting.

Futura Lt BT
COPYRIGHT 1990-2001 BITSTREAM INC. ALL RIGHTS RESERVED.

COPPERPLATE GOTHIC BD BT
COPYRIGHT 1990-2001 BITSTREAM INC. ALL RIGHTS RESERVED.

Vivaldi
URW SOFTWARE, COPYRIGHT 1993 BY URW

PRINTED IN THE UNITED STATES OF AMERICA

January 19, 2007
July 3, 2007
Revised 2009, 2011

Acknowledgments

This book is dedicated to my wonderful husband, John, without whom none of this would have been possible.

Special thanks go to Cami, Cheryl, and Dolly for their prayers, prodding, patience and proofing, as well as Fred, who asked me to write it down in the first place. Also, a big thanks to Clint, who made the inside look great and to Nathaniel who made the outside look fabulous!

∿ God's Gift ∿

This study is based on becoming a woman of faith. "Faith in what?" you may ask. The answer would be: in Jesus Christ. God created mankind to have a relationship with Him. He created husbands and wives to have good relationships with each other to build healthy families, and that is the goal of this book. But unfortunately, men and women, and husbands and wives sin. God sees our sin and because He is absolutely holy, He must judge our sin. He rightfully judges that our sins have earned us eternal punishment and separation from Himself. But since God created us for a relationship with Him and loves us, He sacrificed His only Son, Jesus Christ, on a cross to pay for our sins. God tells us that if we just believe that Jesus died in our place, for our sins, that we are then adopted as His sons, that our relationship with Him is restored, and that we will have eternal life with Him forever. It is a gift from God to us. It costs us nothing.

When we believe, God fills us with His own Spirit, a Spirit of power and of strength so that we can follow Him. If you have not yet accepted God's incredible gift of eternal life through His Son, I pray that you would do so now. The principles in this study are based on believing that God's Word is true and applicable and that God can work in us through His Holy Spirit. It may be harder to understand and apply these principles without faith in Christ, but even so, I pray that your marriage would be blessed and you might come to know God through the concepts presented here.

(Read Romans 3:23, Romans 6:23, Romans 5:8, John 3:16 and Ephesians 2:8-9)

Preface

Dear Ones,

My husband and I like to joke that he has been married to two wives; the wife he married twenty years ago and the remake he got about 5 years later. He prefers the remake.

This is the story of how God most mercifully changed our marriage for the better. He didn't do it by changing my husband, He did it by changing me. You will have your own story; this is mine.

My goal is to share how God changed me, showed me things in the Bible that directly related to what I was thinking and taught me principles that make or break a good marriage. My hope is that my story will lead you to God and that you too will find your answers in His Word and seek to live life as He has planned, not as the deceiver of this world would prefer.

My prayer is that you will find a better way to live with the wonderful man God has given you or if you are not married, the wonderful man He is preparing for you.

Sincerely,
Deborah Chapman

Table of Contents

CHAPTER 1:
Where to Start?

I'm not sure where to start, but usually it is wise to set a goal. I'm going to assume that your desire, your goal, is to improve your marriage. You may be like me in that you don't believe in divorce, but you wish you did, so that you could escape from an unhappy, unfulfilled marriage. I felt very bitter, misused and trapped at the beginning of the story. God was able to change that. It wasn't painless. I felt like my heart and thinking were totally ripped asunder and then carefully and painfully stitched back together into a new pattern. But it was worth it. Just ask my husband if you don't believe me.

In order to produce a more healthy marriage, we must follow the guidelines that God set forth thousands of years ago. The problem is that we are sinners, we don't like following God's ways, and we are being deceived about what makes a marriage work by the ruler of this present age. You might be in a marriage situation where you feel you have to do, initiate and watch over everything in order for things to turn out right. You might be thinking that if God would just change *(fill in the blank)* in your husband, then everything would be alright. You might have been praying and praying that God would change that thing in your husband. You might be thinking that you can't make your marriage work by yourself.

The truth is, you can't make your marriage work by yourself. You also can't expect your husband to spontaneously and miraculously change into whatever you have in mind. But *God* can change your marriage, I believe for the better, when you let Him change *you*. Your husband doesn't even have to be in on the process.

Let's start with an illustration. Imagine with me, if you will, a small stream joyously bouncing down a hillside. It is sparkling, clear and fresh. As it tumbles over small pebbles and rocks, you can hear a soft murmuring and the splashing droplets catch the sunshine like a thousand diamonds. You know that over time it will continue to rush down the hill, broadening and slowing until it becomes a true river feeding the ocean. This is like the sparkling freshness of a new marriage—full of light and promise with only small pebbles to overcome.

Now imagine that the stream is a little bigger and older and that the day is cloudy and cold. There are not small pebbles and rocks to go over, but huge boulders. The water pounds against them and the soft murmuring has become a loud roar. There is no light to catch the spray, only muddy banks to feel each cold drop as it seems to hit and hit in the same spot. Life is cold and bleak and there seem to be no answers. This may be an older marriage, and the light has fled.

Now let us consider what two things are constant about these pictures. The first is that there is water, and it must run downhill. That is how God made it to run. The second is that there are rocks and boulders, and they help to determine the course and path of the river. I want to suggest that in our marriages, our husbands are like the water. Our husbands will and must determine a course for us and our families, just as the water will and must flow downhill. We wives are like the rocks, either blocking the stream or helping to guide it. But unlike the rocks on a bank which must be pushed and rounded and broken by the force of the water because they do not have the option of moving on their own, we, as living stones, can move and change ourselves, through God's strength and direction, to direct the flow of water into a smoother, calmer and more soothing channel. Now you might think I am suggesting that the wife should take a leading role in her marriage. Nothing could be further from the truth. But I am suggesting that we as wives can have incredible influence, as God changes and moves us, to change the flow and nature of our marriages. We have the ability to make it a roaring torrent, crashing against boulders of our own pride and stubbornness, or to make it a calming flow, gently rubbing against our rough spots. Our husbands, like the water, will continue to be the persons they are, and will take us and our children in the direction that they want to take us, but we, unlike the rocks, don't have to fight and resist their course and direction. We can allow God to transform *us* and move *us* to change the flow, and God doesn't have to change the water at all. It can change just because we have changed. It depends on where and how you place the rocks.

> ☙ WE CAN ALLOW GOD TO TRANSFORM US
> AND MOVE US TO CHANGE THE FLOW
> OF OUR MARRIAGES. ☙

Just like the river illustration, our marriages and families can be looked at as systems. Each person is a part of the system and influences the system. Imagine a teeter-totter with two people sitting on it going up and down quite easily. If one person picks up a heavy stone or shifts his position on the teeter-totter, the effort or position of the other person must also change in order to keep going up and down easily. Since our marriages and families can be looked at as systems, any significant change in a family member can precipitate a change in the marriage/family system. If your husband were to change his work hours, then the family schedule might have to shift. If you added another child to your family, it is likely that the family dynamics would have to adapt and adjust to the new member. So too, if you transform the way you look at and live life, then it is possible that the way you and your husband interact might also be transformed. Unfortunately, change is generally difficult and systems often prefer to return to their previous states. But if we allow God to change us into the women He designed us to be, our husbands will have greater freedom to change the way in which they respond in our marriages. The marvelous part, the freeing part, is that once we realize that it is not our job to change our husbands, then we can concentrate on what God wants to do in *us*, and that is enough for anyone.

Further Study for Chapter 1:

Just as our marriages are systems, so are our lives as we relate and interact with others, especially God. God desires that His children, those who have believed in the death, burial and resurrection of Jesus for their sins, seek Him and trust Him. As we begin this study together, read and meditate on 1 Peter 2:1-6.

What does God want us to put aside?

What does God want us to do?

What do we look like in His sight?

What is God building with us living stones?

If we believe in Him, what shall we not be?

N I AM SO LOOKING FORWARD TO THE BLESSINGS THAT GOD WILL HAVE FOR US AS WE SEEK HIM THROUGH HIS WORD AND TOGETHER BUILD OUR SPIRITUAL HOUSE. N

CHAPTER 2:
The First Fall

In the beginning, God created. He created everything, from the tiniest particles of matter, to the huge expanses of the universe. He determined how to split the heavens and the earth, how far the oceans would go before they had to stop, and how silly the ostriches would be when they stepped on their own eggs. He measured the heavens out with the span of His hand and knows how many grains of dust He placed on the planet. He created the angels and the archangels. He created man a little lower than the angels and put the world into subjection under his feet. What an incredible God we belong to! But He also created free wills. He allowed angels and men to choose those things which they would do, and then in ways I will never understand, He works all those choices, both good and bad, into His ultimate and final plan for His creation.

In the beginning, God created, and in the beginning, there was rebellion. There was someone who thought they had a better idea. God tells Ezekiel about it in Ezekiel 28:12-17.

> "Son of man, take up a
> lamentation for the king of Tyre,
> and say to him, "Thus says the Lord God:
> You were the seal of perfection,
> Full of wisdom and perfect in beauty.
>
> You were in Eden, the garden of God;
> Every precious stone was your covering;
> The sardius, topaz, and diamond,
> Beryl, onyx, and jasper,
> Sapphire, turquoise, and emerald with gold.
>
> The workmanship of your timbrels and pipes
> Was prepared for you on the day you were created.
>
> You were the anointed cherub who covers;
> I established you;
> You were on the holy mountain of God;
> You walked back and forth in the midst of fiery stones.

You were perfect in your ways
from the day you were created,
Till iniquity was found in you.

By the abundance of your trading
You became filled with violence within,
And you sinned;

Therefore I cast you as a profane thing
Out of the mountain of God;
And I destroyed you, O covering cherub,
From the midst of the fiery stones.

"Your heart was lifted up because of your beauty;
You corrupted your wisdom for the sake of your splendor;
I cast you to the ground,
I laid you before kings,
That they might gaze at you."

This was written about the real King of Tyre, the king of a major shipping and trading port, but it is also usually considered to describe Satan. Looking at it in that context, then, this is Satan; the mighty Lucifer. He was created by God to be someone really special. He was perfectly formed and walked in Eden and on the holy mountain with God. He was beautiful and wise and walked in God's perfect ways. God had made his plan, his creation, and sealed it up with his final seal of approval, which was Satan. He had a place of honor.

But something happened. Satan's heart, the heart of the one who was a covering cherub and was very close to God, became full of pride. I can only guess at what happened, but I can imagine that in his very important job, he became proud in his power and greedy for the things that he manipulated. He began to see the power of things, rather than the power of his relationship with God. He became so blinded by his quest for objects and the power that they could give him that he decided that he could do without God. He could create his own place and his own rules, through whatever means he needed, including violence, to get what he wanted. Ezekiel says, "Your heart was lifted up because of your beauty; You corrupted your wisdom for the sake of your splendor;" Somehow, Satan must have thought that because he was so beautiful and so wise, that he could be better than the very One who created him. He wanted to do things *his* own way. He wanted some of the power he was so close to. Therefore, God says, "I cast you to the ground, I laid you before kings, that they might gaze at you." (Ezekiel 28:27) Ezekiel goes on to predict his ultimate end and destruction, but that hasn't happened yet. For now, Satan roams the earth and has many titles and much power.

The cast down Satan is a demon of destruction. He still fights against God today, and considers it victory when he blinds or deceives someone to the truth or causes a believer to stumble or rebel. That is why it is written of him,

> "Be sober, be vigilant; because your adversary the devil walks about like a roaring lion, seeking whom he may devour." (1 Peter 5:8)

How does he choose to devour and kill? Some would suggest that he goes around to individuals, constantly attacking them. Thus the expression, *"The devil made me do it."* We need to realize, though, that his power as "the god of this age" (2 Corinthians 4:4), "the prince of the power of the air" (Ephesians 2:2), and the ruler "of the darkness of this age" and "the spiritual hosts of wickedness" (Ephesians 6:11-12) would lead him to wage a much more comprehensive and hidden war. He is "a liar and the father of it" (John 8:44) and the "ruler of this world" (John 14:30). As such, his weapons will be deception and a world system of thinking that will trick and capture mankind into degraded living, slaves to his lies unless men choose to trust God and live according to His Word.

SATAN'S GOAL IS TO TRAP US IN MISERABLE LIVES SO THAT WE CANNOT OR WILL NOT LOOK TO GOD FOR ANSWERS.

Satan's power, the power to set up world systems and kingdoms and fraudulent ways of thinking, will be very important as we try to discover exactly how we are blinded and tricked in our understanding of marriage. In Genesis 1:26-27, God says,

> "Let Us make man in Our image, according to our likeness; ...So God created man in His own image; in the image of God He created him; male and female He created them."

God's image is reflected in the marriage relationship. If Satan can damage and destroy marriages, then he has succeeded in damaging God's image in this world. If Satan can trap us into miserable lives so that we cannot or will not look to God for answers, then we cannot be light and salt to others, showing them how God's ways really do work.

I want to leave this with a final passage from Isaiah. Think about the last line of this. I believe it is the key to how we have been deceived, and why we choose our own sinful way.

> "How you are fallen from heaven,
> O Lucifer, son of the morning!
>
> How you are cut down to the ground,
> You who weakened the nations!
>
> For you have said in your heart;
> 'I will ascend into heaven,
> I will exalt my throne above the stars of God;
> I will also sit on the mount of congregation
> On the farthest sides of the north;
> I will ascend above the heights of the clouds,
> I will be like the Most High.'" (Isaiah 14:12-14)

Satan's sin, the one he was cast out of heaven for, seems to be that he wanted to be equal with God. He wanted to be like the Most High, with all of the power, responsibilities and decisions that go with it. Basically, he wanted to do things his own way. For that, he lost his position, is trying to win his battle with God through his victories over us, and will ultimately be punished forever and ever. He wanted his **own way**; he wanted to **be like the Most High**.

Further Study for Chapter 2:

Read the story of David, a man after God's own heart, in
1 Chronicles 21:1-15.

Why did David order a census?

Who tried to talk him out of it?

Because of David's sin, 70,000 Israelites died.

>  WHEN WE FOLLOW SATAN,
> WE TREAT HIM AS THE "MOST HIGH"
> AND OTHERS SUFFER.

Read the story of Christ in Luke 4:1-13.

Who led Him in the wilderness and who else was there?

Why could Satan offer Christ the kingdoms of the world?

Did Satan succeed in the temptation?

Because of Christ's faithfulness, all men can be redeemed.

>  WHEN WE FOLLOW GOD,
> WE RECOGNIZE HIM AS THE "MOST HIGH"
> AND OTHERS ARE BLESSED.

CHAPTER 3:
The Second Fall

We change scenes now to the Garden of Eden. God has finished His creation, has taken His Sabbath rest and now walks in the garden daily with Adam. He gives Adam one command, saying,

> "Of every tree of the garden you may freely eat; but of the tree of the knowledge of good and evil you shall not eat, for in the day that you eat of it you shall surely die." (Genesis 2:16-17)

It seems simple enough. The garden is loaded with beautiful, bountiful trees, and succulent, delicious plants, every one of them fit for a feast and ready for Adam and Eve to gather and eat. They only have to stay away from one tree. Now if God had not ever wanted to deal with sin, He would not have put the tree in the garden. But He did plant the tree and He gave Adam complete instructions about it.

Adam and Eve shared a wonderful relationship, for none other than the Almighty God had put them together, they are naked and not ashamed, they can communicate with God and one another freely, completely, and understandably, and life is good. Adam has told Eve of God's command and she knows very well the tree that she is not to eat from. Now enter the serpent of old, who "was more cunning than any beast of the field which the Lord God had made."(Genesis 3:1) He approaches the woman and starts questioning God's commands, just as he did when he was cast down. He was probably still very beautiful, so that Eve may have been pleased and intrigued by his lovely appearance.

> "And he said to the woman, 'Has God indeed said, "You shall not eat of every tree of the garden"?'"(Genesis 3:1)

He was trying to trick her into a simple yes, and to get her to think about all the trees in the garden.

> "And the woman said to the serpent, 'We may eat the fruit of the trees of the garden; but of the fruit of the tree which is in the midst

of the garden, God has said, "You shall not eat it, nor shall you touch it, lest you die.""" (Genesis 3:2-3)

We can see at this point Eve knew that that tree was off limits. Now we don't know whether or not Adam had told her not to touch it or not, but she knew that God didn't want her eating from that tree. Eve could tell from Satan's first statement that he knew about God's rules. He knew the tree and that God had given them a certain command against it. As he continues his conversation with her, he very cleverly inserts one big lie into some more truth.

"Then the serpent said to the woman, 'You will not surely die. (*A lie.*) For God knows that in the day you eat of it your eyes will be opened, and you will be like God, knowing good and evil. (*The truth.*)'" (Genesis 3:4-5)

In Eve's bedazzlement with the serpent, and her conversation, she lost track of one very important fact. She was already like God because she was made in His image. Genesis 1:26-27 tells us that God said,

"Let Us make man in Our image, according to our likeness; ...So God created man in His own image; in the image of God He created him; male and female He created them."

Eve was already like God, although she momentarily forgot it, but Satan tempted her with the same sin that had cast him out of heaven. He told her she would be like God, just as he desired to be "like the Most High." What a thought for her, to be like God. She saw God every day and was able to talk with Him without falling on her face in terror and fear of His righteousness and glory. I wonder what she thought it would be like to be like God. I bet at that point she ceased to be content with what she had.

The story continues in verse 6.

"So when the woman saw that the tree was good for food, that it was pleasant to the eyes, and a tree desirable to make one wise, she took of its fruit and ate."

Satan was able to appeal to Eve and deceive her at all points where we are tempted. In 1 John 2:16, John writes,

> "For all that is in the world--the lust of the flesh, the lust of the eyes, and the pride of life--is not of the Father but is of the world."

Satan is the prince of this world, he has already been cast down, and he has set up the world system for his purposes. He knew exactly how to deceive Eve. He offered her the lust of the flesh, it "was good for food," the lust of the eyes, it was "pleasant to the eyes," and the pride of life, it was "desirable to make one wise." Satan had set up the system, he knew how to use it and he had his first victim. "She took of its fruit and ate." I don't know about you, but my heart sinks within me when I think of that simple, yet devastating act.

The story continues with, "She also gave to her husband with her, and he ate." I've always wanted to know more about this part. Was Adam standing beside her listening in on her whole conversation with the serpent or did she just come prancing up to him somewhere else in the garden and hand him the fruit? The point is, however, that he must have known what fruit she was presenting to him, because when God judges the man, He says,

> "... you have heeded the voice of your wife, and have eaten from the tree of which I commanded you, saying, 'You shall not eat of it.'" (Genesis 3:17)

For Adam to have heeded the voice of his wife, rather than obeying what God had commanded, he was knowingly sinning.

> ♪ WHEN THEIR PRIDE AND DESIRE
> TO BE LIKE GOD CAME,
> THEY ATE AND WERE ASHAMED. ♪

At this point in the story, all the relationships fall apart. Adam and Eve realize that they are naked and shame enters the world. Proverbs 11:2 says that, "When pride comes, then comes shame;". When their pride and desire to be like God came, they ate and were ashamed. Then came the work. They had to try and cover-up what they had done. They tried to make clothes out of fig leaves. After that, they had to hide. It is hard to hide from an all-seeing God. Then they had to sound nonchalant as they called out from their hiding place. At this point, Adam and Eve are on the same team. They are working together to cover up what they have done. But when it is discovered, their unity is dissolved and the blaming begins.

> "And He said, 'Who told you that you were naked? Have you eaten from the tree of which I commanded you that you should not eat?'
>
> Then the man said, 'The woman whom You gave to be with me, she gave me of the tree and I ate.'
>
> And the Lord God said to the woman, 'What is this you have done?'
>
> The woman said, 'The serpent deceived me, and I ate.'" (Genesis 3:11-13)

In this short passage, Adam blames God for giving him a woman, he blames the woman for giving him the fruit and Eve blames the serpent for deceiving her. It is every person for him or herself and it's his or her fault. Alas, just as sin came down from Adam, so too has blaming and fault finding in our marriages.

For Further Study Chapter 3:

Carefully read Genesis 1:26 – 3:24.

Record any thoughts or insights you might have.

CHAPTER 4:

The Results of the Second Fall

At this point God has to pronounce judgment on all involved. God curses the serpent and offers a glimmer of the future Messiah. Then He moves on to the woman.

> "To the woman He said:
> I will greatly multiply your sorrow and your conception;
> In pain you shall bring forth children;
> Your desire shall be for your husband,
> And he shall rule over you." (Genesis 3:16)

Besides the need for pain management classes for childbirth, we now have power struggles built into our marriages. Our *desire* shall be for our husbands. The Hebrew word for desire in this passage is *"teshuwqah."* It means a stretching out after or a desire to run after or over, or a longing to overflow, as with water. It can also mean an attempt to usurp or control. It is only used three times in the Bible: Once here, once in Genesis 4:7 and once in Song of Solomon 7:10. Let us start in the middle and work backwards. In the Song of Solomon, verse 7:10, it says, "I am my beloved's and his desire is towards me." This would seem to indicate that her lover has the desire to run after her and to make her his own, to conquer her.

The 2nd use of *teshuwqah* in Genesis 4:5-7 says,

> "but He did not respect Cain and his offering.
> And Cain was very angry, and his countenance fell.
> So the Lord said to Cain, 'Why are you angry? And why has your countenance fallen? If you do well, will you not be accepted? And if you do not do well, sin lies at the door. And its *desire* is for you, but you should rule over it.'"

Cain has just had his offering rejected by God, while his brother's was accepted. He was angry, but God clearly told him that sin was crouching at his door, ready to run after him, to overwhelm and conquer him. I always imagine sin in this passage as a lion crouching just ahead of him ready to pounce on him and tear him to pieces. But whatever picture you see, the word *desire* clearly has the connotation of something trying to control, to overwhelm and to gain the advantage over Cain. Sadly, he gives in to it and the first murder occurs, but that is another story.

Using this illustration, let's see how it might apply to the woman's judgment. Our desire, our *teshuwqah*, shall be for our husbands. Using our newly found understanding of the word desire, we could rewrite it to say: *Our longing is to run after, to overflow, and to control our husbands.* One of the biggest obstacles to a godly marriage is our desire to have the last word, the final say, the authority over our husbands. But God doesn't allow us to have our own perverted way, because He continues the judgment with, "He shall rule over you."

The word rule in this verse is the Hebrew word, *"mâshal."* It means to rule, to have dominion, to reign or to have power. It is the same word used in Genesis 1:17-18 where it says,

> "God set them in the firmament of the heavens to give light on the earth, and to rule over the day and over the night, and to divide the light from the darkness. And God saw that it was good."

The sun and the moon have the power to reign over the day and the night. That is the way God created them. So too, even though we *desire* to have the power in our marriages, God declares that our husbands *will* have it. That is God's judgment. Because of the second fall, not only will our marriages contain blaming and fractured relationships, but they will also have power struggles. The wife will *desire* to control her husband, usurping his authority, questioning his decisions and trying to get things *her* way, but the husband *will* have the final say. Even if our husbands are not following God or leading their families well, they still have the *power* in the marriage relationship and will resist any attempts from us to dominate them. God did not judge the man's *ability* to be the leader, the head of the household or the final authority in the marriage. He *will* be the leader. We, as women, just want his job.

Understanding this, I want to go back to the illustration of the stream. God has designed our husbands to go the way He wants them to go. Our judgment means that we want to say how, when and where he goes, and in our desire to have control, we will put ourselves in front of our husband to try to block his way, to change his course. The only result is extra friction and noise in our marriages as our husbands have to beat against us with roaring power to get to the place they want to take us.

Further Study for Chapter 4:

Read 2 Samuel 6:12-23.

*Did David and Michal have different
ideas about how David should conduct himself?*

Who won?

What were the consequences of the power struggle?

Now is where it starts getting personal.

*Can you think of a time you were in a
power struggle with your husband?*

Who won?

What, if any, hard feelings or consequences resulted on either side?

CHAPTER 5:

Me? I Don't Want to Rule.
I Just Want to Fix My Husband

Now, you may be thinking that you would never try to rule over your husband or get your own way. You may be thinking that you love him just the way he is. But if you are like me, you may have thought that just maybe he could change one or two little things and then everything would be wonderful and you would be happy. Or maybe you have a whole wish list of things you would like to change in your husband. Of course, we are easily deceived by the semantics, and our desire to transform our husband into our ideal of the model husband is just another phrase for trying to get *our* own way by ruling his life. Perhaps you are reading this as you are preparing for marriage. If so, this applies to you too. Just put, fiancée, into the husband slot, and truly consider what plans you have for your life together.

> *♪* OUR DESIRE TO TRANSFORM AND RULE
> OVER OUR HUSBANDS IS JUST ANOTHER WAY
> OF TRYING TO GET OUR OWN WAY. *♪*

Let's take a closer look at this. It is important. I want you to make a list. It will have two parts. In the left column, I want you to make your own Top 10 list of all the things you have ever tried to change in your husband. (No one else needs to see this list, so get it all out. You don't have to have ten, or you may have more.) After you have finished, fill in the right column, beside the thing that you wanted to change in him, the way in which you went about it.

What I have tried to change in my husband:	How I have gone about it:
1.	1.
2.	2.
3.	3.
4.	4.
5.	5.

What I have tried to change in my husband:	How I have gone about it:
6.	6.
7.	7.
8.	8.
9.	9.
10.	10.

Read over what you have just written. Does anything repeat itself or does there seem to be a theme? If so, write it here.

My hope is that your list is short, and that you have chosen to try and change your husband by lifting him up in prayer before God. Unfortunately, your list, like mine, may be long and ugly. When I first did this, years ago, my list looked like this:

What I have tried to change in my husband:	How I have gone about it:
1. Be a self-starter	1. Go ahead and start my work and show bad temper by being sullen and resentful.
2. Be less of an impulse buyer	2. Remind him of his allowance and that I am no longer working.
3. Automatically respond to unspoken pleas	3. Become sullen and resentful-- "Why doesn't he understand and respond?"
4. Be ready to work when I am, even if he'd rather read a book	4. Resentful and silent
5. Get rid of the dog	5. Nagging, complaining
6. Be more of a leader when I'm indecisive	6. Impatient
7. Want to do things when it is convenient for ME.	7. Begrudging of his time

God used my list to hit me right between the eyes with some very unpleasant truths about myself. I was being foolish by hoping my husband would respond to things he didn't even know about, and I was being selfish, since most of the things I wanted to change in him were things that would serve me. But the biggest hit to my wonderful opinion of myself was the way in which I chose to respond to my husband. Not only was I ignorant of the fact that it was not my job to change my husband, but my method for trying to change him was sullen, nagging, impatient resentment. No wonder I was unhappy. This seemingly simple mental exercise had shown me my heart, and it wasn't a pretty sight.

Proverbs 30:21-23 says,

"For three things the earth is perturbed, yes, for four it cannot bear up; For a servant when he reigns, a fool when he is filled with food, a hateful woman when she is married, and a maidservant who succeeds her mistress."

The whole world order is shaken when a woman full of hate is married. If you hate or disrespect your husband, it has serious consequences. One of the major reasons for hating your husband is resentment and anger towards him. The following chapter may not be as pleasant as some of the others, but until we surrender our resentment towards our husbands to God and let Him deal with our hearts and our husbands, we will never be able to move any closer to our goal of a satisfying marriage. Please linger until you have dealt with your resentment. It is a huge stumbling block, one the Deceiver wants to use to keep us broken, bruised and bleeding.

Further Study for Chapter 5:

Read Psalm 139:1-6

What does God already know about your attitudes, actions and reactions towards your husband?

Read Proverbs 16:2, Proverbs 21:2, and Jeremiah 17:9-10

What do we generally think about our own actions?

What does God know of them?

Are we sometimes blind to our own motives?

CHAPTER 6:

Understanding Anger and Resentment

Proverbs 21:9 "Better to dwell in a corner of a housetop, than in a house shared with a contentious woman."

Proverbs 21:19 "Better to dwell in the wilderness, than with a contentious and angry woman."

Proverbs 27:15 "A continual dripping on a very rainy day and a contentious woman are alike."

James 1:20 "...for the wrath of man does not produce the righteousness of God."

Solomon seemed to understand, as he penned the book of Proverbs, how awful it is to try and live with an angry and bitter wife. If we, as wives, don't deal with our resentment, we may drive our husbands out of the house, either literally or figuratively. No matter how they try to get away, the result will be the same, an unhappy marriage. I can't stress enough how important it is to learn how to deal with this problem in our lives. So, let's begin.

N IF WE DON'T DEAL
WITH OUR RESENTMENT,
WE MAY DRIVE OUR HUSBANDS AWAY. *N*

First, let us look at some of the causes of anger. I will suggest three broad categories, you may have others. The first is a blow to our pride. When someone accuses us, attacks us, or makes us look or feel bad, we become offended and angry with them, because they have dared to prick our pride. This can have serious consequences as seen in the Biblical examples of Joseph and his brothers. The brothers could not handle the fact that Joseph might rule over them. After all, he was the youngest and ought to know his place. Because they were jealous and resentful, they sold him and shipped him off to Egypt as a slave. (Genesis 37) Or what about Saul and David? Consider what happened to Saul's heart when he heard, "Saul has killed his thousands, but David his tens of thousands." (1 Samuel 18) What did Nebuchadnezzar do to Shadrach, Meshach and Abednego when they defied him by not bowing down to his image? (Daniel 3) How did the Jews respond to Stephen when he told them that they, perfect as they were, were the ones responsible for Christ's death on the cross? (Acts 7) He wounded their pride; they stoned him for his honesty.

The second broad category for inciting anger is to cross someone's will. When Moses came to free the Israelites from bondage, he crossed the will of Pharaoh which was to have them continue as slaves. God gives us several chapters in Exodus telling about the destruction and chaos that resulted from Pharaoh's anger at having his plans interrupted. Do you remember Balaam the prophet and his donkey? The donkey tried to protect Balaam from an avenging angel, one that Balaam couldn't see, by stepping out of the path or by stopping. All he received from Balaam for his efforts was cursing and beating. Balaam was angry that his donkey would not keep going in the path that he, Balaam, had chosen. (Numbers 22:21-35) Balaam's tune changed when God showed the angel to him, but his initial response to his donkey getting in his way was anger.

The last broad category has to do with our expectations. This one is not quite as clear-cut as the first two, but I believe it causes much resentment in our families. Often, we get angry when someone doesn't perform or treat us in the way that we anticipated that they would. We see this when Naaman the leper asks Elisha the prophet how to be cleansed from his leprosy. Elisha tells him to go wash in the river seven times. Now, I'm sure that Naaman was expecting something far more complicated and impressive than washing in the river seven times. He became angry about it, but when he was finally persuaded to wash, God healed him in spite of his nasty attitude. (2 Kings 5:1-19) We have seen how Saul railed at his own son Jonathan for befriending the man who was the greatest threat to Jonathan's chance for the throne. (1 Samuel 20) Saul couldn't understand why Jonathan wasn't as greedy for the kingship as Saul expected him to be, so he responded in anger.

Now comes the difficult part: Looking at your own heart. Can you think of instances in your own marriage in which you have become angry because your husband pricked your pride? Did he ever correct you in front of someone else? Criticize you for your housekeeping or cooking skills, or lack thereof? Did he ever compare you unfavorably to someone else? Perhaps it was a thoughtless remark about your attire that stung you. I'm sure the list of ways our pride can be hurt is longer than I could ever begin to write down. Now comes the real question: Are you still carrying the anger, resentment or hurt of that situation in your life and attitude? What do you do about it?

What about a crossing of your will? Can you think of instances in your marriage in which you didn't get your own way? What about times when you didn't let your husband get his own way? Do you think that there might be unresolved anger and resentment over those situations still poisoning your life and attitudes? What do you do about it?

What about unmet expectations? How do you respond when he does not come home on time? When he says he will do something and then doesn't? What if he doesn't spend as much time with you and your children as you feel he ought to? What if you've made plans based on the accomplishment of some specific action by him, and then he doesn't do it? Not only has he not met your expectation, but he has also crossed your will. Do you still carry feelings of helplessness and rage in the wake of your frustrated expectations? What do you do about it?

〜 HAS YOUR PRIDE BEEN HURT?
HAS YOUR WILL BEEN CROSSED?
HAVE YOUR EXPECTATIONS BEEN MET?
WHAT DO YOU DO ABOUT IT? 〜

Generally, we get mad. Our countenance falls. We gather ammunition against our spouse by dragging up past incidents and mulling over them so that we feel justified in our anger. We start to blame our spouse for everything that goes wrong, while being blind and deceived about our own part in it. We begin to rationalize our own actions in self-defense. Our anger begins with the problem. As we continue to dwell on the problem, we start to see it as a result of character flaws in our husband. From that blame and resentment, it is a short hop to questioning our relationship with our husband. We start to internalize all these feelings and let them ferment in our minds like a pot of sourdough starter, working, seething, growing, just waiting to bubble over. Then comes the "great confrontation", when we finally blow and unload days, weeks or years of bilious anger on our unsuspecting spouse. The confrontation may make us feel better for the moment, but it can cause lasting resentment, hatred, distance, bitterness, discouragement, spiritual darkness (1 John 2:9-11), and regret in our marriage.

Think about your own marriage. Are you full of unresolved issues and conflicts? Do you have any way to deal with them? This would be a very depressing chapter if the answer to that question was no. Fortunately, we do have another choice. Read on.

Further Study for Chapter 6:

Read Genesis 4:1-16.

Where did Cain's anger start?

How did it develop?

What was the confrontation like?

What were the consequences?

CHAPTER 7:

Anger is a Choice

Anger and resentment are choices. Galatians 5:19-21 would say they are choices of our flesh. But we are now children of God and we are to walk in the Spirit.

> "But the fruit of the Spirit is love, joy, peace, longsuffering, kindness, goodness, faithfulness, gentleness, self-control. Against such there is no law. And those who are Christ's have crucified the flesh with its passions and desires. If we live in the Spirit, let us also walk in the Spirit. Let us not become conceited, provoking one another, envying one another." (Galatians 5:22-26)

Let me repeat part of that verse, "...and those who are Christ's have crucified the flesh with its passions and desires." Our desire, our *choice*, when we hold on to our anger and hold grudges and issue ultimatums to our husbands, is one of the flesh. So what do we do with it? The Bible would tell us to crucify it, to put it to death. But that means you have to decide that you truly want to be rid of it. Some of you may not be miserable enough to want to let go of your bitterness. My prayer is that God will make your life so unpleasant that you will have no other option than to follow Him and decide to do things His way.

So, how do we crucify our anger? We start by choosing to take up our cross and follow Christ. We must take our pride, our rights, our own plans and our expectations and we must nail them to the cross. We must change our focus from ourselves to Christ, to His example, His commandments, and His power within us through the Holy Spirit. We must *choose* to change. Here is where this process gets personal, painful and profitable. Personal because it deals with our inmost heart, painful, because we have to set aside our own pride, agenda, and self will, and profitable because we gain Christ, the righteousness which He desires in us by faith, and hopefully, a renewed marriage.

Let us begin by looking at the example of Christ. He came to this world from heaven to live like a man. That means He left the comfort and glories of heaven just so he could go through the process of being born, of growing up, of dealing with siblings and the teasing of friends and enemies. He had to endure the adolescent years of growing and change, and then had to set out on His own, (probably to the disappointment of Joseph who would rather have had his step-son follow in his footsteps) and find new friends. For three years, there was constant traveling on hot, dusty, rough roads, with poor accommodations, and ceaseless demands for miracles, teaching, blessings, and food. The end came with the final dramatic entrance into Jerusalem and a season of unimaginable horror and pain as those He came to save tortured, beat and mocked Him.

If anyone had a reason for pride, it was Jesus, who created all things, and without whom, "nothing was made that was made." (John 1:3) He suffered blows to His pride when his parents didn't understand why He would be in His Father's house, and when the priests in charge of His house plotted to get rid of Him.

If anyone had a reason to get His own way, it was Jesus, who knew the heart and plans of His Heavenly Father, and who would never make *any* poor decision. He knew that everything He did was for the good of someone else, and yet man kept trying to interfere and make Him do things *his* way.

If anyone had a reason to expect good things from the people God created, it was Jesus. He and the Father had given man everything needed for an abundant life, and yet we refused to listen, refused to see the good, refused to honor God as we turned aside, everyone to his own way, to wallow in our own pride and despair. But what did Christ do when He had every right to be disappointed and angry? He decided to forgive. He let God the Father deal with the sin when He said, "'Father, forgive them, for they do not know what they do.'" (Luke 23:34)

In the same manner, we must decide to forgive. First, decide that you have had enough. Decide that you are willing to get rid of your anger, resentment and grudges against your husband. Then start praying. I always like to think of King Hezekiah when he received threats from the King of Assyria about being taken over. 2 Kings 19:14-16 says,

> "...and Hezekiah went up to the house of the Lord, and spread it (*the letter of threats*) before the Lord. Then Hezekiah prayed before the Lord, and said:
>
>> 'O Lord God of Israel, the One who dwells between the cherubim, You are God, You alone, of all the kingdoms of the earth. You have made heaven and earth. Incline Your ear , O Lord, and hear; open Your eyes, O Lord, and see;...'"

Likewise, you can take your list of complaints about your husband, either written or mental to the Lord. Spread it out before Him and ask Him to hear and to see what you have been storing in your heart. Tell Him that you have decided to be rid of it. Tell Him that you need to crucify it and for Him to take the burden of it from you. Humble yourself before Him, confess your sin in holding on to it, and ask Him to take it from you and to strengthen you in His Spirit to dwell on those things which are

> "...true, whatever things are noble, whatever things are just, what ever things are lovely, whatever things are of good report, if there is any virtue and if there is anything praiseworthy -- meditate on these things." (Philippians 4:8)

Ask God to give you the strength and power to forgive your husband for any past wrongs, real or imagined, so that your actions toward him will match your decision to forgive. Then you will follow in the way of the child of God as written in Colossians 3:12-17,

> "Therefore, as the elect of God, holy and beloved, put on tender mercies, kindness, humility, meekness, longsuffering; bearing with one another, and forgiving one another, if anyone has a complaint against another; even as Christ forgave you, so you also must do.

But above all these things, put on love, which is the bond of perfection. And let the peace of God, rule in your hearts, to which also you were called in one body, and be thankful.

Let the word of Christ dwell in you richly in all wisdom, teaching and admonishing one another in psalms and hymns and spiritual songs, singing with grace in your hearts to the Lord.

And whatever you do in word or deed, do all in the name of the Lord Jesus, giving thanks to God the Father through Him."

This exercise in forgiveness may be really tough the first time, because we may have a long list of stored resentments to forgive. Unfortunately, because we are sinners, we will have many more situations in which to practice our faith-following-Christ-in-forgiveness decision, and it will not necessarily get any easier. But we must remember, when new grievances or hurts come to mind, to continually *choose* to forgive. Then, and sometimes even harder, we must try to forget, to stop dwelling on the offense, to put it behind us, and to *act* as if we have truly forgiven our husbands.

True change occurs in our lives when our basic *thinking* has changed. Prior to God showing me my heart, I would have an emotional response to whatever my husband did or didn't do. I would behave badly toward him based on my feelings at the time. I rarely thought about the consequences of the resentment and bitterness that I was bringing into my marriage. But when we read God's Word and realize what He really wants us to do, then we can begin to live our lives differently. If we understand that acting on our negative feelings can produce frustration in our marriages, and we take time to *think* correctly about our anger and the destructive fruit it will produce, then we can choose to crucify it, to put it aside. Once we have put it aside, then we can choose to *act* on our new thinking. For example, even though we may have forgiven our husbands for something they did, it often seems hard to forget it and put on a new emotional face towards them. That is when we can act on our new thinking by replacing the poisonous thoughts we had towards our husbands with those that are true and of good report. When we substitute thoughts of things that we love and admire in our husbands for the angry thoughts that we had previously, we will be learning to dwell on the things that God talks about in Philippians 4:8, and by the time we get to the tenth thing that we admire about our husbands, it becomes much harder to be bitter toward them. Instead of acting on our feelings, we must choose to act on our new thinking, and then correct feelings can follow.

We MUST DECIDE TO FORGIVE, ACT UPON OUR DECISION AND LET CORRECT FEELINGS FOLLOW. *

Now that you have decided to be free of your anger by handing it off to God, and you have forgiven your husband from your heart and put on new love for him, then it is time to tell him. Go to him with a repentant spirit, confess your anger and wrong attitudes, tell him you have forgiven him, and that you desire to change the way that you respond to him. Don't try to manipulate him or put him on the spot by asking for forgiveness from him. He may offer you forgiveness, but don't expect it. He probably will not understand your new thinking and new attitudes until he sees how you act and react toward him in the future.

If you say you have forgiven him, but don't act like it, he will probably think you were just trying to manipulate him. If, however, he sees your actions matching your words, then, because our marriages are systems, he will be more likely to learn a new way to react to the new you.

WHEN GOD BEGINS TO CHANGE YOU AND YOU LET GO OF YOUR BITTERNESS, DON'T EXPECT AN IMMEDIATE RESPONSE FROM YOUR HUSBAND OR FAMILY. *

When God begins to change you with your decision to let go of past bitterness, don't expect great, immediate responses from your spouse or family. The first adjustment has been made to the system and it will take time for the new you to affect the whole. Just as when you change the position of one part of a hanging mobile, the final positions of the whole mobile will not be determined until it stops swaying. So also will the final response of your husband not be determined until he sees your new freedom from anger and your new love for him. Don't base your desire to change on an expectation of change in your husband, because he may disappoint you and choose not to change. Learning and living new patterns of behavior is hard work, and most systems resist permanent change. But God is pleased when we obey Him. Therefore base your desire to forgive, to love, and to change on the peace God promises, because He never disappoints.

Further Study for Chapter 7:

Read James 1:19-25

What are we to be slow to do?

What does our anger NOT produce?

*If we effectively **do** what God requires of us, what will happen?*

Consider your own marriage.

Are there issues in it that need to be addressed and forgiven?

If so, consider this your invitation to pray about them, to confess them, to choose to crucify them, to ask for forgiveness for them and to put them aside, acting in love towards your husband. Then, be amazed at the incredible work God will do in your life as you follow Him and love your husband.

❧ LET US BE BLESSED AND UNSTAINED BY THE WORLD BY CHOOSING TO FORGIVE AND ACTUALLY DOING IT. ❧

CHAPTER 8:

What Does All This Have to Do With Me and My Marriage?

It may seem like we are taking a very roundabout road to discussing our marriages. We have talked about Satan's fall, man's fall, the consequences of the fall, and the need to crucify our resentment and put on love. But you may want to know what you are supposed to do. Why haven't we come to the main point of wives in the home? Because it is important that we understand why things are the way they are.

If Satan hadn't desired to be like God and hadn't been cast down to the earth to rule it and to set in place his own twisted ideas of how life should work, we wouldn't have any reason to be deceived about what God really desires for us. If we hadn't seen man's fall and its consequences, we wouldn't have realized that women are easily deceived and that we desire to run things our own way. If we hadn't looked at the destructive power of anger and resentment, we would not understand the need to crucify our anger and to forgive our husbands. God, when writing His book through Paul in the epistle of Colossians, doesn't begin to address the roles of people in the home until forgiveness, love and thanksgiving are in place. The passage about putting on tender mercies, longsuffering, forgiveness and love comes immediately before the verses which deal with the role of wives, husbands and children. In other words, Colossians 3:12-17 comes right before Colossians 3:18-21,

> "Wives, submit to your own husbands, as is fitting in the Lord. Husbands, love your wives and do not be bitter toward them. Children, obey your parents in all things, for this is well pleasing to the Lord. Fathers, do not provoke your children, lest they become discouraged."

If one time is not enough to convince you, look at the end of the fourth, the fifth and the beginning of the sixth chapter of Ephesians. There Paul writes that we are to put off the old man and put on the new man which was created according to God. He writes that we are to put away lying and wrath, that we are to

"...Be kind to one another, tenderhearted, forgiving one another, even as God in Christ forgave you." (Ephesians 4:32)

We are told to be imitators of God, to walk in love, to put off the life of the darkness and to walk as children of light, and that we are to speak to one another

"...in psalms and hymns and spiritual songs, singing and making melody in your heart to the Lord, giving thanks always for all things to God the Father in the name of our Lord Jesus Christ, submitting to one another in the fear of God. (Ephesians 5:19-21)

Paul writes these things right before Ephesians 5:22-24,

"Wives, submit to your own husbands, as to the Lord. For the husband is head of the wife, as also Christ is the head of the church; and He is the Savior of the body. Therefore, just as the church is subject to Christ, so let the wives be to their own husbands in everything."

and Ephesians 5:33,

"Nevertheless let each one of you in particular so love his own wife as himself, and let the wife see that she respects her husband. Children, obey your parents in the Lord, for this is right ...fathers, do not provoke your children to wrath, but bring them up in the training and admonition of the Lord."

Maybe God knows it is important that we deal with our rancor, and come to a place of singing and thanksgiving in our hearts *before* we try to live with our husbands in a godly manner. Maybe God knows that our antagonism towards our husbands has to be dealt with before we can follow Him by submitting to our husbands.

N GOD KNOWS THAT WE MUST DEAL
WITH OUR ANGER BEFORE
WE TRY TO LIVE WITH OUR HUSBANDS
IN A GODLY MANNER. *N*

Further Study for Chapter 8:

Read Colossians 3:1-17

What are we to seek? (1)

What does verse 3 say?

What is happening to our new self? (10)

When we forgive, what should we put on? (14)

What should rule in our hearts? (15)

What should richly dwell within us? (16)

How should we do all that we do? (17)

CHAPTER 9:
What is a Wife to Do?

(1 Corinthians 11:3) "But I want you to know that the head of every man is Christ, the head of woman is man, and the head of Christ is God."

(Ephesians 5:22-24) "Wives, submit to your own husbands, as to the Lord. For the husband is head of the wife, as also Christ is the head of the church; and He is the Savior of the body. Therefore, just as the church is subject to Christ, so let the wives be to their own husbands in everything."

(Colossians 3:18) "Wives submit to your own husbands, as is fitting in the Lord."

(1 Peter 3:1) "Wives, likewise, be submissive to your own husbands,..."

What is the theme of these verses? Wives be submissive to your own husbands. This idea of submission is one that generally sends fear and trembling into the heart of every modern, "liberated" woman. Most women at first glance assume that to submit means to obey without question and to be doormats and slaves. That's exactly the connotation that Satan would love to have us believe, for if we do, we will live in fear of our husbands and as rebellious, defeated, conquered wives. But we are easily deceived. God does not call us to be slaves to our husbands; He calls us to submit to our husbands, *as to Him*. If we are willing to follow and submit to Christ, then we should be just as willing to follow and submit to our husbands. Let's look a little closer at what that really means.

First of all, let's define what submission isn't. Submission isn't just strict obedience. I know of women who have told me that they were submitting to their husbands by obeying them while gritting their teeth in rebellion and hate. Obeying because you feel compelled to without willingness or respect is not submission. It is slavery. Slaves don't obey necessarily because they *want* to, but because they *have* to; they are slaves. If we feel we *have* to obey our husbands, and obey begrudgingly without respect or love, then we are acting as slaves and our actions in our marriage might look like, *"I'll do it, because I have to, to be a 'good, submissive wife', but I'll show him. His plan will fail, especially if I have any say in the matter. Just you wait and see."* God never called us to be slaves to our husbands. He has called us to freedom through His truth: Freedom from sin, freedom from anger and freedom from all the attitudes that hinder our walk with him. (John 8:31-36) That is why God tells us to put off the old self with its bad attitudes and put on the new self with forgiveness, longsuffering, love and thanksgiving, *before* He tells us to walk according to His plan. It may be, that if your attitude toward submitting to your husband is poor, that maybe you haven't fully dealt with some anger or resentment from the previous chapters. If you think submission is obedience with a bad attitude, think again.

ϟ IF YOU THINK
SUBMISSION IS OBEDIENCE WITH A BAD ATTITUDE,
THINK AGAIN. *ϟ*

At the beginning of 1 Peter 3:1, it says, "Wives, likewise, be submissive..." That likewise means in like manner or in the same way as. In the same way as what, you may ask. Well, it refers to the previous verses in 1 Peter, chapter 2 where it talks about Christ and His attitude when He had to suffer unjustly. Jesus is our supreme example of submission under pressure. I'm sure if Jesus had His way, He would not have left heaven. I doubt He wanted to sweat, to be hot, tired, and dusty. He would not have wanted to be tempted. He would not have wanted to be tortured and killed in a public and excruciating way. But He considered it important to follow His Father's way, to redeem you and me. He *willingly*, and *with a good heart*, **chose** to follow God the Father's decisions, with nothing but love in His heart, even though He did not deserve the pain it would entail. It says He did not threaten, lie, revile, complain, whine, resent or do it because He "had to" with a sneer, it says He subjected His own will, of His own free choice to the Father's will for the good that would come later. Luke writes that Jesus knelt down and prayed, "Father if it is Your will, take this cup away from Me; nevertheless not My will, but Yours, be done." (Luke 22:42) If He is to be our example, then we also are to willingly, of our own free choice, with love in our hearts, submit to our husbands' decisions, even if our submission may be painful, and even though we have no guarantees of a better life with our husband if we submit.

The word submit has many synonyms. Here are just a few: abide, accede, acknowledge, acquiesce, agree, appease, bend, bow, buckle, concede, defer, give way, humor, indulge, knuckle, lay down arms, obey, relent, relinquish, surrender, truckle, yield. Think on these words as we try another illustration.

I want you to imagine a medieval castle. In that castle is a king. Kneeling before him is one who is desirous of becoming his knight. This would-be knight has trained and studied hard to come to this place and now he must willingly kneel before his king. He is not forced to kneel, nor is he being held down by guards. He has chosen to kneel before his king who is holding a sword. In the traditional ceremony, the king will lightly tap the knight on each shoulder, accepting his offer of service and putting himself in authority over that knight. At this point, the knight is in a position of high vulnerability. If the king chooses, he could chop off the knight's head as easily as tap him on his shoulders. The knight, at this point, has chosen to submit himself to his king, trusting that his king will use him well in his service for good and not for evil, and the king as he taps his knight must trust that the knight will not one day turn the sword back towards him or against him for evil. This knight is acknowledging before all those present that the king is his king. He is ready to agree with the king's decisions, he is willing to bow before him and to humor, indulge and give way to the king's wishes before his own. He has chosen to yield his own will and relinquish his own rights for the benefit of the king. We might all agree that this is a beautiful picture of what should be right and good in the kingdom, and that as the king makes good decrees and the knight carries them out, the kingdom and the people will prosper. This is a picture of submission that carries with it a heart attitude of willingness and trust.

⚘ SUBMISSION IS A CHOICE BASED ON TRUST. ⚘

When we choose to submit ourselves to our husbands, we are putting ourselves in a place of high vulnerability. Just as the king while holding the sword over the knight is in a position of great power over that knight, so our husbands will have great power over us if we choose to submit ourselves to them. When we willingly invest our love and efforts into serving them, they have the option of accepting our service for good, or rejecting it and wounding our hearts. Here is a trust issue. Do you trust that your husband will treat you well if you willingly choose to submit to him? If so, then your response to one of his decisions might be more like, *"Sweetheart, I'm not sure that I agree with what you have decided, but I know that you love me and want only the best for us. I know that God will take care of us in all your decisions, so not my decision, but yours is the right one, and I will do everything in my power to abide by it and support you."* This is not just the slavery of obedience with spite, this is godly submission. What's the difference? **The difference is the attitude.**

Now, I realize that acceding to your husband's decisions and submitting to him with a heart full of love might leave you open to ridicule, disbelief and scorn from those around you who have no idea about what God really planned for our lives, and it seems like an all-win situation for your husband, but think on this last benefit.

When God put his plan of life into place, He created it with order. He established the first governmental system, or hierarchy. God the Father is over everything. Christ is first after Him. Husbands are to be under Christ, and wives (and children) are under the authority of the husband. Just as a supervisor is responsible and accountable to *his* boss for the actions and decisions of his employees, so must our husbands

be responsible and accountable to Christ for the things that *we* do. That means that even if we, as wives, choose to overrule our husbands, and to implement plans that are outside the boundaries that they have set for us, that our husbands are still accountable for our actions. (1 Kings 21) What an awesome responsibility our husbands have! They must answer to God for their families. They are to provide direction, instruction, and protection for us before God, and one day they will have to stand before the Lord and give an account of their leadership in the family. If they have truly done what God has asked them to do, it will go well with them, but if they have not led and their family has suffered, then those consequences and loss of rewards will be on their own heads. God will judge our husbands for their leading and decisions.

> ∿ GOD WILL JUDGE
> OUR HUSBANDS FOR THEIR
> LEADING AND DECISIONS. ∿

But what about the wives? Are we exempt? Indeed not. We also will have to present ourselves before God to give an account of our actions and attitudes in the family. As long as we, as wives, have submitted to our husband's authority and have willingly accepted his care and protection, then it will go well with us because honored his authority. But if we choose, of our own accord, in our own will, not to accept our husband's leading and direction, then we will have placed ourselves out from under his care and will be directly responsible and accountable to God for our actions. When the time for judgment comes, not only will God take us to task for not submitting to our husbands, but He will also judge our husbands more severely because of our actions. I do not want to be the cause of more judgment on my husband because I refused to submit to him, do you?

> ∿ GOD WILL JUDGE
> US ON HOW WELL WE
> SUBMITTED TO OUR HUSBANDS. ∿

God will judge our husbands for their leading and decisions, whether right or wrong, but He will judge us on how well we submitted to those decisions. How much easier and better it is for us to simply follow our husbands and trust God for our care.

Further Study for Chapter 9:

Read Genesis 18:19. God just announced to Abraham that he and Sarah would be the parents of a son within the year. Through Isaac, God would establish a great and mighty nation in which all the earth would be blessed.

Why did God choose Abraham?

Read Ephesians 5:22-33.

What does verse 22 tell us to do?

Verse 25 tells husbands to love their wives just as what?

List the things Christ does for the church in verses 25-27.

What are husbands to do for their wives in verses 28-29?

If our husbands love us as God commands in verses 25-29, would they ever do or decide anything to cause us harm or hardship?

WHY, THEN, ARE WE SO UNWILLING
TO LET THEM LEAD?
WHY WOULD WE EVER BE UNWILLING
TO BE SUBJECT TO THEM?

CHAPTER 10:
The Incredible Power of A Woman

Oh yes, I know that this submission discourse sounds easy on paper, but it isn't the same in actual practice. *"I don't like submitting!"* *"I don't want to do that!"* *"I should have some say."* *"I am important too!"* Because we want to be "like the Most High", and because of the Genesis 3 judgment, that is just what we want to say. God's judgment affected our ability to follow willingly and with a good attitude, our *followship*, if you will. Since we want to be in control, and we want the *authority*, we do not make good followers. But what I want to suggest, is that, although we do not have the authority in the home, we do have incredible influence. Even though we do not have the authority to make the final decision, we do have the power to determine the way in which that decision is manifested. In some ways, our influence may be more potent than the authority, specifically in determining the mood of the home and the members in it. The old saying, *"If Mama ain't happy, ain't nobody happy,"* is not very far off the mark, for it has to do with the emotional influence of Mama, not just her decisions. Our followship, or lack of it, has an incredible power to determine the timbre of the home and those who dwell in it. Let's look at some illustrations which might help to make this plain.

I have heard that women's influence in the home is like a small rock, wedging under a large boulder on a hill. The picture continues with the exhortation that if we, as women, would just get out from under the boulder, our husband, that he would be able to roll the way he wanted and everything would be just fine. That interpretation is right up to a point, but I think it falls short of depicting our true influence. I don't think it even begins to address the emotional side of the way we follow in the home.

Let's try another picture. Imagine your husband as a general. You are the sergeant and everyone else is the troops. The general gives an order, expecting the sergeant to activate the troops, so that they as an army can go out and win the battle. There is only one tiny problem. The sergeant doesn't like the general's order and so doesn't tell the troops or follow the general's order. In fact, what is even worse, the sergeant may even bad-mouth the general behind his back to the troops. The general can't go out and win the battle by himself; he needs the rest of his army behind him. He can try talking to the troops directly, but they will be confused, because the sergeant is not going off to battle, and they want to know why she doesn't have to go along too. The troops are confused and demoralized, the general is frustrated, and the battle can be lost, all because the sergeant thought she had a better idea. It wasn't that the general did not have the authority to give the command, rather it was the lack of following which lost the day. In the armed forces, the result would be court martial. In our families, the results can be chaos, confused and angry children, and/or divorce, whether legal, spiritual, emotional or physical. But that might be too convicting, so let's move on.

As you consider this next illustration, I want you to empathize with the driver of the wagon. I want you to put yourself into his shoes and let yourself feel emotionally what he might feel.

Imagine a wagon. On the front seat is the driver, in front of him is his mule, hitched to the wagon, and in the back of the wagon are his two children and his crops. He has to get the crops to town, so that he can sell them and get flour, sugar, etc. It is a long way to town and he must arrive before the stores close in order to have time to trade his goods. He gives the order to gee-up to the mule, and the mule just stands there. He tries the command a little more forcefully the second time. This time the mule looks back at him over its shoulder and brays. He gives the command a third time, this time with just a slight pop from his whip. The mule brays more loudly and sits down. The driver becomes frustrated and exasperated as the minutes pass and he can't get the mule to go. He climbs down from the wagon and tries coaxing it, gently stroking its back and speaking nicely in its ear. He might have been speaking softly to a rock for all the good it does him.

He might try a carrot for a reward, although he surely doesn't feel like rewarding the mule. He might try force, pulling on the bridle or pushing on its rear end. He might try ranting or raving. Whatever action he takes, his heart is filling with anger and frustration, he knows time is running short, the kids are getting worried, cranky, and whiny and he would probably rather go beat his head against a wall than to have to try and deal with this mule. If he ever succeeds in getting the mule to go, and even if he and his family finally get everything done, he will probably end the day exhausted, frustrated, mad, resentful and definitely harboring no love toward his mule. Unfortunately, that mule is probably his wife, resisting him at every point, trying to get him to do things her way, and blocking him from doing the things he knows are right to do. No wonder our husbands are angry people. They have to deal with stubborn wives.

> ✿ No wonder our husband's get angry.
> They have to deal with stubborn wives. ✿

So, why are we so stubborn? Why aren't we willing to follow even when our unwillingness destroys our marriages and families? Why do we sacrifice joy-filled, abundant home lives for our own pride? It goes back to the sin and judgments of the first and second falls. We want to be "like the Most High." We want our own way, and not only that, we want our own way over our husbands' way. We are a sinful people driven by our own desires. Fortunately, God loves us and can help us, in spite of our sin, if we are willing.

> "But God demonstrates His own love toward us, in that while we were still sinners, Christ died for us." (Romans 5:8)

Since God gave His Son to die for us, we have an out. We have a way to conquer our own sinfulness. It is by trusting that Christ died for our sins, and by trusting that the power that God used to raise Christ from the dead is at work in us through the Holy Spirit. We must realize "that just as Christ was raised from the dead by the glory of the Father, even so we also should walk in newness of life... Therefore do not let sin reign in your mortal body, that you should obey it in its lusts. And do not present your members as instruments of unrighteousness to sin, but present yourselves to God as being alive from the dead, and your members as instruments of righteousness to God. For sin shall not have dominion over you, for you are not under law but under grace." (Romans 6:4,12-14)

We have a great Savior and a great God, Who fills us with His glorious Spirit when we believe. With all these things going for us, we can succeed in changing ourselves, if we will crucify our sinful attitudes and present ourselves to God. We can give our desire to control our husbands to God and ask Him to give us submissive hearts and minds. We can trust Him to do the work, *but only if we are truly willing to give up our own control.* It is a matter of faith. It is a matter of trust. Do you truly believe that God is strong enough, wise enough, and willing enough to take care of you if you choose, from your heart, to obey Him by doing things His way, and not your own?

N DO YOU BELIEVE THAT GOD
IS BIG ENOUGH TO TAKE CARE OF YOU
IF YOU CHOOSE TO OBEY HIM AND DO LIFE HIS WAY? *N*

Further Study for Chapter 10:

According to the <u>American Heritage Dictionary</u>, faith is "a confident belief in the truth, value or trustworthiness of a person, idea or thing." It is also a "belief that does not rest on logical proof or material evidence."

Read Ephesians 2:8-9

How were you saved?

Was it a result of your own works or your own efforts?

Read Colossians 2:6-10

According to verse 6, if you received Christ by faith, how are you to live or walk?

According to verse 8, how can we be taken captive or cheated?

Who set up the principles or teachings of the world?

In verse 10, it says that in Christ we _____.

Being in Christ means that we trust Him, confidently believing that what He says is true. When we walk and live by faith in Christ, we are complete and full.

If we trust Him and follow our husbands because He asks us to, will that make us empty or incomplete?

Would you rather live as a captive to Satan and his worldly principles, or would you rather live and walk by faith in Christ, doing what He asks, trusting Him and your husband, even though there is no tangible proof that everything will work out well?

WALK BY FAITH.
TRUST CHRIST TO GIVE YOU
THE ABILITY TO FOLLOW YOUR HUSBAND
AND TO TAKE CARE OF YOU.

CHAPTER 11:
Are We Done Yet?

Now you may be thinking that we are done. We've taken tremendous steps to get rid of our past resentment and anger toward our husbands, and we've suffered through yet another lecture on submission. We have all the knowledge we need to go out and change the world, one marriage at a time. But one question that we haven't asked, or answered, is this: Other than the fact that God has said men should rule, is there any reason that women shouldn't run things? After all, we are not necessarily stupid or incompetent. Women have fought for a long time in America to get equal rights. Some think that Thomas Jefferson should have included *"and women"* in his phrase, *"...all men are created equal..."*. If you ask them, many men in America will be glad to tell you how much better their wives run things than they do. After all, we truly desire to rule.

Let's start by looking at some Biblical examples of women ruling. Then we can decide, based on the evidence, whether or not it is a good idea. The places to look are found with the phrase, "He heeded the voice of his wife." To heed means to listen to, to consider. I want to look at a few examples of Biblical couples where the woman had a great idea, proposed it to the man, he heeded it, acted upon it, and chaos followed.

Our first example, of course, has already been discussed. In Genesis 3:17, Adam "heeded the voice of his wife" and ate of the fruit. Eve had a really bad idea, and when Adam deferred to her, sin entered into the world. Notice also, that God let Eve off as "being deceived", but her husband, Adam, is the one who had to accept the responsibility for his actions and those of his family. He is the one of whom it is written,

> "...through one man sin entered the world, and death through sin, and thus death spread to all men...", "...by the one man's offense many died...", "...the judgment which came from one

offense resulted in condemnation..." and "...by the one man's offense death reigned through the one..." (Romans 5:12,15,16,17).

What a legacy Adam left to the world from heeding the voice of his wife.

Genesis 16 tells us the story of Abram, Sarai and Hagar, Sarai's Egyptian maid. God had promised to make Abram a great nation, but to do that you need to have children. Sarai was barren and had no children, so she had a great idea. Abram should use her maid as a surrogate mother, Sarai would have her long wished for child, and Abram could be the father of a great nation. "And Abram heeded the voice of Sarai." (Genesis 16:2) He went into Hagar and she conceived, then Hagar began to despise Sarai. Then comes the ironic twist to the story. Sarai, instead of being overjoyed, and having a wonderful time with her plan, now sees how foolish it really was, and starts blaming Abram.

> "Then Sarai said to Abram, 'My wrong be upon you! I gave my maid into your embrace; and when she saw that she had conceived, I became despised in her eyes. The Lord judge between you and me.' So Abram said to Sarai, 'Indeed your maid is in your hand; do to her as you please.' And when Sarai dealt harshly with her, she fled from her presence." (Genesis 16:5-6)

Sarai is not seen in the best of lights in this particular passage. She knew that God had promised Abram and her many descendents. She had already waited 10 years for God to fulfill His part of the bargain, but still she was childless. She was getting old and was desperate for a child. She wasn't willing to trust God; she thought He needed a little help. She thought she had a better idea than what God had in mind. After all, hadn't He promised them a child? Well, she probably thought it didn't matter how the deed was accomplished, so she came up with Plan B. Hagar would have a child for her. Abram probably knew it was a bad idea, but to get her off his case, he "heeded" her voice and got Hagar pregnant. Hagar looks down her nose at Sarai and

Sarai realizes that Plan B was not all it was cracked up to be. She blames Abram for making it happen and Abram instead of settling it between the two women just washes his hands of the whole mess and tells her to do what she wants. That's what she has been doing so far, she might as well continue. Sarai is so unkind to Hagar that Hagar leaves. Then God talks to Hagar in the wilderness by a spring, tells her to go back and be nice to Sarai, and tells her some interesting things about her son. Since Abram is his father, and Abram is to be the father of many nations, this child will have many descendents. The bad news is that, "He shall be a wild man; his hand shall be against every man, and every man's hand against him. And he shall dwell in the presence of all his brethren." (Genesis 16:12) This son, this wild man would be the father of the Arab peoples, and he will always be against others. Even today, thousands of years later, the sons of Ishmael and the sons of Isaac are still fighting. How much bloodshed in Arabian wars throughout history would have been avoided if only Abram had not heeded the voice of Sarai?

Sarai, now Sarah, finally had the promised son, Isaac. He married his cousin, Rebekah and they had two sons, Esau and Jacob. While they were still in the womb, Esau and Jacob used to fight. Rebekah asked God about it, and He told her that there were two nations in her womb and that the older would serve the younger. Now it seems that Isaac loved Esau, the oldest, best, but Rebekah loved Jacob, the younger, more. When Jacob was over forty years old, his mother overheard Isaac promising to bless Esau. She had her own ideas about who ought to get a blessing, after all, God had promised that Jacob would be the prominent son, so she embarked on a sneaky, deceitful plan to steal Esau's blessing from him. Jacob went along with it and so heeded the voice of his mother, even though he was quite old enough to have said she was wrong to suggest such a thing. His only contribution was to make sure that every possible precaution was taken so that the plan would succeed. He did receive the blessing, but he also had to run for his life and never got to see his mother again. God had promised Rebekah that the older son would serve the younger, but she didn't allow Him to do it in His way. She thought she had a better idea. One of the most amazing things to me in this story is how God used her sinful action to bring about His righteous plan. I'm sure He could have and would have handled it on His own if she had given Him time, but even in spite of our doubts and lack of trust, God can still bring His plans to fruition.

I'm sure there are more examples of women who had a plan, and their husbands heeded them, but I want you to see some critical points, points that will and can apply to us.

✒The first is that **these women had clear instructions and/or promises from God:** Eve knew about the tree, Sarai was promised many descendants, and Rebekah was promised that Esau would serve Jacob.

✒In spite of the clear instructions, **these women didn't trust that God would do what He said:** Eve didn't trust God's withholding of the tree from them for their own good, Sarai didn't trust that God was able to supply the promised child without her help and Rebekah didn't trust God to give Esau and Jacob the right blessings.

✒Next, **these women decided that they had a better plan:** Eve decided to get wise without God's help, Sarai decided to have a child through Hagar, and Rebekah decided to trick Isaac to make sure he would give the best blessing to Jacob.

✒**These women carried out their plans, overruling their husbands:** Eve gave to Adam to eat and he ate, Abram got Hagar pregnant, Rebekah tricked Isaac and carried Jacob along with her plan.

✒**They and others lived to regret their actions:** Sin entered the whole world through Adam, the Arabs will always fight the Israelis, and Rebekah never got to see Jacob again.

The point is this: **When these women overruled their husbands, in distrust of God, bad things happened.**

N **WHEN THESE WOMEN
OVERRULED THEIR HUSBANDS,
DISTRUSTING GOD,
BAD THINGS HAPPENED.** N

The long and the short of it is that we still desire to be "like the Most High." We still want our own way.

Further Study for Chapter 11:

Stop here and think. Was there ever was a time when you overruled your husband? Was it about something that you had been promised or that you thought was important to your family? Were you tired of waiting for your husband to do it, and tried to take matters into your own hands? Did you "talk your husband into it," or force him to agree? Were the results what you expected? Did you, your husband or others suffer because of your poor choice? Did you, as Sarai, blame your husband for carrying out your plan because you didn't like the results of your poor decision? If so, describe it now.

The results of an ungodly or distrustful wife who interferes with God's plan for marriage and the family can be horrible and longstanding. Consider this verse in 1 Kings 21:25 that talks about one of the worst kings of Israel.

> "But there was no one like Ahab who sold himself to do wickedness in the sight of the Lord, because Jezebel his wife stirred him up."

🖊 DO YOU EVER STIR UP YOUR HUSBAND TO ACT UNWISELY OR IN AN UNGODLY MANNER BECAUSE OF YOUR DESIRE TO RULE? 🖊

CHAPTER 12:
I am Fallible

So, how do we put aside the desire to rule...

                     ... how do we learn to follow?

The first step is to understand that women are imperfect. We are more easily deceived than men, otherwise, Satan would have gone to see Adam. Women *can* be wrong.

For me, learning that I could be wrong was a big step in God's plan for changing me. After all, I was smart. I got a full ride scholarship to the school of my choice in Colorado because I was a good student and active as a leader in many school organizations. I graduated with High Honors from one of the best engineering schools in the country. Within two years of graduating, I was in a management position with my company and on the fast track to bigger and better things. I made the "noble sacrifice" to stay home with our children when that time came, but even so, I was sure I could run our home *and* my husband just as well as I ran things at work. I had not yet come to the point in my life, like Paul, where I considered all my righteousnesses as filthy rags and desired nothing but to know God. I was still secure and trusting in my own pride, intelligence and competency when God chose to teach me that I could be wrong and that I was not as trustworthy as I thought.

One of the first times I came face to face with my own fallibility was when I saw the list of the things I wanted to change in John. Through my own sinful responses, I was forced to see *myself* as being the one at fault and the one deceived about my thoughts and attitudes. I found out that I could be wrong, and I was not nearly so worthy of my trust as I believed myself to be. Our pride takes a big blow when we are not right, and when we try to rule and are not right, as in the case of Eve, Sarai and Rebekah, it can be disastrous.

Let me look back and give you three examples from my marriage to try and show you the process of how my desire to rule, to be "like the Most High", to always be right and to trust only myself changed to an understanding that I could be wrong and maybe I should trust someone other than myself. I'd like for the examples to be extremely profound and enlightening, but they are actually pretty mundane. Bear with me, for hopefully, they will help to illustrate how this simple, yet far reaching concept of self-distrust and God-and-husband-trust works.

After John and I had been married a year or so, and we were both working full-time, I was having trouble keeping up with all the housework. We agreed that one night a week, on Thursday, he would be responsible for dinner. He could take us out, he could pick something up, or he could cook. The problem started the first night he decided to cook. I stayed in the kitchen to watch. Now I already knew that he was a fairly good cook, but I didn't trust him to be alone in the kitchen. I had to be there to tell him where things were, and to make sure I could answer any questions he might have. I wanted him to cook me a meal, but I still wanted to control the way he did it. It didn't matter that he was very capable of cooking it in his own way, which was different from mine, but just as effective. All that mattered to me was that he do it *my way*.

God's pronouncement about wanting to rule over my husband was very much present in my kitchen on Thursday nights. John managed to get tasty meals on the table, but by the 3rd or 4th time he cooked, there was real tension in the kitchen. I wanted him to cook my way, I didn't want him to get extra dishes dirty, I didn't think that he should stir that in such and such a way, etc. He finally agreed to cook only if I left the room entirely. I did not trust my husband enough to cook me a meal. I only trusted myself. After that, I simply went to the den and read a book till he called me for dinner, and I kept my mouth shut about the mess in the kitchen. At that point, I simply avoided forcing my will on him, but I certainly didn't understand it or try to deal with the root problem of lack of trust.

Move the clock ahead a few years. We now had one child, we had moved to West Virginia, where the nearest family was seven and one-half hours away, I was a full-time mom, having left my job in Colorado, and John was making noises about possibly wanting to go into the ministry some day. He had always wanted to be a pastor, but he had never felt called to be a pastor. I had never wanted to be a pastor's wife, and was not very thrilled with the prospect of having to go through lean seminary years and all the moving and changing involved afterward. I was very comfortable being the wife of an up-and-coming geologist. But, I knew I had to support my husband in whatever decision he and God made, since God was the one who would do the calling. I just assumed that that calling would come soon and that John would no longer be able to support me.

I didn't think that God was big enough to take care of us, so I decided I had better take things into my own hands. I called my sister, who was a home-sales cosmetic consultant and helping to support her husband through seminary, and had her sign me up. I would sell cosmetics to the women of West Virginia and we would be all right. Now, I don't know how much of this John realized. I think he thought I was just bored with being a full-time, stay-at-home mom. Bless his heart, he didn't complain, rebuke, or try to talk me out of it, he just supported me in my lack of trust. After a year of missing evenings with my husband and child, and trying to keep up with inventory and ordering during my son's naptime, and piling my laundry room shelves with pink boxes of cosmetics, I was tired. I missed spending time with my family, the financial rewards were just not what I thought they would be, and I called it quits. If God wanted John to go to seminary, He certainly was not going to be helped by my annual profit that year, which was $23.81. I was still clueless about the real motives behind my decision to try and sell cosmetics, but I did realize that my plan had not worked, no matter how hard I tried, or how well I had thought it out. This was a first step in my journey of realizing that perhaps I was fallible. Maybe I wasn't always right. I had always been right before, but this was one of my first failures. It was a good thing, too. It planted those first seeds of self-doubt, that maybe I wasn't as trustworthy as I thought.

Move ahead only a year or so. We had a second child now, I was resentful of my husband, and had been going through a course on renewing my marriage to try and find a way to fix us. I had just seen my bad attitudes in the "What do I want to change in my husband list" and so was not so cocky and sure of myself as I once was. I had not gotten too far into the rest of the course, but I knew with my head that I was to submit to my husband. I knew that it meant I had to go along with whatever he decided. It didn't mean I was to be a doormat, or that I couldn't have any input, but that I was to support his decision, whether or not I agreed. I knew this was an obedience issue, not to John, but to God.

God said I was to submit, accede, bend, defer, surrender, etc. *my way* to my husband's, *with a sweet spirit*, not grudgingly or looking for revenge later. I was still very much struggling with the idea that John was to have control, but I was so miserable and so convicted by the Spirit, that I was willing to step out in faith and try obeying what God's Word said. This was a decision based on changed thinking for me, not one based on emotions. All my emotions were saying, "Whatever you do, keep control! John is sure to make a wrong decision, and then where will you be?" But I now knew that God would hold me accountable for my decision to obey Him or not. He would hold John accountable for the decision on the issue. This is what I knew, and had decided, and God was swift to try my faith.

> *ⁿ* OBEYING GOD AND MY HUSBAND
> WAS A DECISION BASED ON CHANGED THINKING,
> NOT ON EMOTIONS. *ⁿ*

Some opportunity came up, it was so trivial, that I have even forgotten what it was now, but there was some important new idea or concept or opportunity that I thought John and I should take part in. I had talked it over with a good Christian friend of mine, and we both agreed that this definitely was the thing to do. I broached it to John when he got home. He totally disagreed. He told me I was wrong, and then he gave me very good reasons why it would not be the thing to do. I remember being amazed at some of the things he brought up during our discussion. He had considered and thought of things I would never have thought of in a million years. He considered not only the here and now, but things past, present and way beyond my immediate world. He was very nice about the whole thing, but firm in his decision. I knew that to fulfill my desire to submit to my husband, I had to genuinely support him in his decision, even though I felt deep in my heart that he was absolutely wrong.

When I saw my friend next, I had to explain to her that we were following John's decision. She asked me all the questions that I had asked John the night before, and I had to give her his reasons to defend his decision. It was incredibly hard for me to defend the decision with my husband's arguments, especially since I did not agree with them, but God, through His Spirit, had impressed on me that it was important that I do this, and with a good attitude. I couldn't defend his decision spitefully or condescendingly, but from the heart. I was very glad to see her go that day.

God, in His gentle mercy, wanted to stress the point, so He gave me the opportunity to go through it all again the next day, with another dear friend, in the same way. By that time, I was so worn out with the whole affair that I didn't care anymore. Of course in a few weeks, John was proved absolutely right, and my Christian women friends and I were proved absolutely wrong. This was a very important moment for me. It was the first time I had come face-to-face with the realization that I could be wrong and *John* could be right. My decision to follow John's way and not my way had turned out right. Now I had even more proof that I was not trustworthy, but even more heartening was the fact that I was married to a man who was.

My esteem and respect for my husband soared as my opinion of my own way plummeted. Many of the self-help books out there would probably scoff at the idea that you are not to trust and esteem yourself and your own opinions, but for me, it was the beginning of better things. I had to learn that I could be wrong. I had to learn that John was almost always right, because he considered and reflected and was aware of things that I would not even be mindful of. This is how God taught me that my husband was worthy of my trust and I, myself, was not. This was also one of the first times that I saw real, distinct proof that God's way, so seemingly foolish to this world's system, actually worked.

♪ GOD AND OUR HUSBANDS CAN BE TRUSTED TO DO WHAT IS RIGHT. ♪

God had allowed me to discover one of the most important concepts for changing our marriages. We wives need to realize that God and our husbands can be trusted to do what is right. Let me repeat that, **God and our husbands can be trusted to do what is right.** God did not design us to be the head: Not the head of the universe, the world, His promises, or our families. Since we are not designed to be in charge, we are not equipped as well as our husbands to make the best decisions. I am still amazed by my husband's thoughts when we are considering a major or minor decision. He continues to weigh facts that I would never think of. I am so glad that he can and will do that, and that he has made so many wise decisions for our family. **But I only began to see his care for me and our family, and began to rely on his trustworthiness when I was no longer trusting myself.** I am not implying that women are stupid, that we do not know or think about things that our husbands need to know, or that we can never have any good ideas or suggestions, but I am saying that we need to come to a point where we no longer trust ourselves to make all the decisions. We need to accept the truth of God's judgment in Genesis, subject our *desire* to rule over our husbands to them and accept their rule over us. We need to trust in our husband's decisions, knowing that they will be accountable to God for them if they are right or wrong.

Now, I know that if you have not yet come to the point of distrusting yourself that you will be asking:

But what if my husband won't make a decision?
What if he makes a bad decision?
My husband is not a good leader.
How can I train him to be a good leader?

 GOD DESIGNED YOUR HUSBAND FROM BIRTH TO BE A GREAT LEADER.

The answer is that God has designed your husband from that first breath of life to be a great leader. He may be out of practice if you have been doing things your way. But if you will trust God to take care of you, and you will rely on the husband that He has given you, then He will take care of you in spite of mistakes your husband may make. **You see, God will hold *you* accountable for the way in which you follow your husband. God will hold *your husband* accountable for his leading, whether good or bad.** And regardless of good or bad leading, if you are doing your job as a helpmate, God will protect you in spite of your husband. We'll look at some examples of that in the next chapter. Come on along!

Further Study for Chapter 12:

Read Proverbs 3:5-8 and Jeremiah 17:5-8.

What happens when we trust the Lord and not ourselves?

 TO TRULY CHANGE INTO THE WOMEN
GOD WANTS US TO BE,
WE MUST DECIDE TO TRUST THE LORD
WITH OUR WHOLE HEART AND TO OBEY WHAT HE SAYS.
IT IS A FAITH DECISION,
ONE THAT IS VERY DIFFICULT TO STEP OUT INTO,
AND ONE THAT CARRIES GREAT REWARDS.

CHAPTER 13:
God's Protection

Let's go back to Genesis. I love this book, because the people are sinful and foolish, just like me, but God continues to work in their lives and carry out His plan in spite of them. Somehow it gives me hope that He can work with my foolishness as well.

In Genesis 12, Abram had just been told to leave his country and family and go to the land that God would show him. God had promised to bless him and make him great. Abram left Haran and his family and went down into Canaan with his wife, Sarai. After a while, there was a famine in the land, so Abram and Sarai had to move to Egypt. Now Sarai, even at 65, was still a beautiful woman, and Abram was afraid the Egyptians might kill him to get their hands on her. So he made the decision to have her tell the Egyptians that she was his sister, instead of his wife. She really was his half-sister, but this seems to be an Abram-saves-his-own-skin-without-regard-to-Sarai type of decision. Sarai heeds the voice of her husband and goes along with the plan. By declaring herself to be Abram's sister, she is now no longer under his protection as a wife. It wouldn't seem to be very safe for her, but she obeys her husband in spite of his decision and ends up being taken into Pharaoh's house. Abram is treated well for her sake, but he doesn't have his wife. God takes care of both of them. He is bigger than Abram's cowardice. He safeguards Sarai from Pharaoh's possible advances, and sends plagues on Pharaoh and his family. The matter is discovered, and Abram and Sarai are sent packing with wealth and gifts from Pharaoh.

Lest you think that Abram learned a lesson, shift forward 24 years. Abram and Sarai have been given new names, the birth of the son of promise was predicted in one year, Sarah and Abraham are now in Gerar, and Sarah is 89 years old. She must still be very beautiful, for once again, Abraham tries to save his neck and tells Abimelech, the king of Gerar, that she is his sister. The king brings her into his house.

Again, Abraham has not made a very good decision regarding his wife, especially since he is supposed to have a son with her within a year, but God, who is always bigger than our poor decisions, takes the matter in hand. This time, God speaks directly to the king in a dream and says,

> "'Indeed you are a dead man because of the woman whom you have taken, for she is a man's wife.' But Abimelech had not come near her; and he said, 'Lord, will You slay a righteous nation also? Did he not say to me, "She is my sister"? And she, even she herself said, "He is my brother." In the integrity of my heart and innocence of my hands I have done this.'

> And God said to him in a dream, 'Yes, I know that you did this in the integrity of your heart. For I also withheld you from sinning against Me; therefore I did not let you touch her. Now therefore, restore the man's wife; for he is a prophet, and he will pray for you and you shall live. But if you do not restore her, know that you shall surely die, you and all who are yours.'" (Genesis 20:3-7)

God has things so much more in hand than we can ever realize. Did you catch His words, "I also withheld you from sinning against Me..."? He knew all about Abraham's poor decision, He directly intervened to keep Abimelech from touching Sarah, and worked quickly to get her back to her husband, so she could have the promised son. He also blessed Abraham through the expensive gifts Abimelech gave him to clear his name and Sarah's name. Abraham prayed to God and God healed Abimelech and his household, and then God visited Sarah with a child as He had said.

In both of these instances, Sarah followed her husband in his decisions. She didn't fight him or betray him. She accepted what he asked her to do and acted completely upon it. Since obeying Abraham pulled her out of his leading and protection, she had to trust God to take care of her. Fortunately, God is always willing to take care of those who trust Him, and He is powerful enough to take care of ugly situations in His own way.

Now for those of you who are familiar with the stories found in the Old Testament, you might be saying to yourselves, "But what about Abigail? She disobeyed her husband, and God seemed to think that it was alright." The story of Abigail and David is found in 1 Samuel 25:2-43. King Saul, the king of Israel, was jealous of David, a mighty warrior who had found favor with all the people and who had been anointed by the priest, Samuel, to be Israel's king after Saul. Because of his jealousy, Saul was seeking David in order to kill him, and David was a fugitive. While on the run, David and his army spent one season helping to protect the large flocks of sheep and shepherds which belonged to a man by the name of Nabal. After the shepherds had brought the flocks in and they had been sheared, Nabal held a feast to celebrate. David sent messengers to Nabal asking for compensation for his protection for the past months. Since it was the end of the shearing, Nabal should have had money with which to pay David and his men, and should have invited them to share in the feast. But Nabal pretended not to know David, denied that David had helped him, insulted David by suggesting that he was a runaway servant trying to take advantage of him, and refused his request. When David's messengers arrived back with Nabal's scornful answer, David and about 400 of his men girded on their swords to slay Nabal and all the males related to him.

Fortunately for Nabal's family, one of the shepherds heard Nabal's harsh message to David and quickly ran to tell Nabal's wife, Abigail, what had happened. She could guess how David would receive the words of her husband, and,

> "Then Abigail made haste and took two hundred loaves of bread, two skins of wine, five sheep already dressed, five seahs of roasted grain, one hundred clusters of raisins, and two hundred cakes of figs, and loaded them on donkeys. And she said to her servants, "Go on before me; see, I am coming after you." But she did not tell her husband Nabal." (1 Samuel

25:18-19)

Abigail met David on the road as he was marching to kill Nabal.

"Now when Abigail saw David, she dismounted quickly from
the donkey, fell on her face before David, and bowed down to
the ground. So she fell at his feet and said: 'On me, my lord,
on me let this iniquity be! And please let your maidservant
speak in your ears, and hear the words of your maidservant.
Please, let not my lord regard this scoundrel Nabal. For as his
name is, so is he: Nabal is his name, and folly is with him!
Now therefore, my lord, as the LORD lives and as your soul
lives, since the LORD has held you back from coming to
bloodshed and from avenging yourself with your own hand,
now then, let your enemies and those who seek harm for my
lord be as Nabal. And now this present which your
maidservant has brought to my lord, let it be given to the
young men who follow my lord. Please forgive the trespass of
your maidservant. For the LORD will certainly make for my lord
an enduring house, because my lord fights the battles of the
LORD, and evil is not found in you throughout your days. Yet a
man has risen to pursue you and seek your life, but the life of
my lord shall be bound in the bundle of the living with the
LORD your God; and the lives of your enemies He shall sling
out, as from the pocket of a sling. And it shall come to pass,
when the LORD has done for my lord according to all the
good that He has spoken concerning you, and has appointed
you ruler over Israel, that this will be no grief to you, nor
offense of heart to my lord, either that you have shed blood
without cause, or that my lord has avenged himself. But when
the LORD has dealt well with my lord, then remember your
maidservant.'" (1 Samuel 25:23-31)

Not only does Abigail disobey her husband by giving David food,
but she speaks of Nabal in a disrespectful manner. David listens to her
plea and accepts the gift she offers.

"Then David said to Abigail: "Blessed is the Lord God of Israel,
who sent you this day to meet me! And blessed is your advice
and blessed are you, because you have kept me this day from
coming to bloodshed and from avenging myself with my own
hand. For indeed, as the Lord God of Israel lives, who has kept
me back from hurting you, unless you had hurried and come to
meet me, surely by morning light, no males would have been
left to Nabal! So David received from her hand what she had

brought him, and said to her, "Go up in peace to your house. See, I have heeded your voice and respected your person." (1 Samuel 25: 32-35)

Abigail knew that she had just saved her husband, and all of his male relatives, but she also knew that she had gone against her husband's wishes and would have to accept the consequences of her actions. She waited until the morning, when Nabal was sober, to tell him what she had done regarding David. She did not take a coward's way out by telling him the night before when he would probably not really have heard her or remembered her words. When Nabal heard what she had done, "his heart died within him, and he became like a stone." (1 Samuel 25:37) Ten days later, God's judgment on Nabal was complete, and he died. David heard of Nabal's death, proposed to Abigail, and she came to him to become his wife.

So, here we seem to have a problem. Abigail clearly disobeyed and disrespected her husband, but God blessed her. Why? How does this fit in with God's instructions about submitting to your husband? Before we answer that, let's look at two other examples, one from the Old Testament and one from the New Testament.

During the reign of King David's grandson, Rehoboam, the nation of Israel split into two separate nations. The northern kingdom was called Israel with the capital in Samaria, and the southern kingdom was called Judah, with the capital in Jerusalem. In 1 Kings, chapter 21, Ahab was the king of Israel, and his palace was located next to the vineyard of Naboth the Jezreelite. Ahab wanted Naboth's vineyard, and offered to swap him some other land for it, or to pay him for it, but Naboth refused, because it was his inheritance, his family's land. Ahab went into his house and sulked, and his wife, Jezebel, asked him what was wrong. He told her that Naboth would not give up his vineyard, and she said,

"You now exercise authority over Israel! Arise, eat food, and let your heart be cheerful; I will give you the vineyard of Naboth the Jezreelite." (1 Kings 21:7)

Jezebel then took command and sent out letters in Ahab's name, which contained a plot to have Naboth killed. When the plot was carried out, and Naboth was dead, then,

"Jezebel said to Ahab, "Arise, take possession of the vineyard of Naboth the Jezreelite, which he refused to give you for money; for Naboth is not alive, but dead." So it was, when Ahab heard that Naboth was dead, that Ahab got up and went down to take possession of the vineyard of Naboth the Jezreelite." (1 Kings 21:15-16)

From what we can read in the account, Ahab does not question Jezebel or her methods, nor does he try to control his wife. She definitely "overrules" him by setting up Naboth's murder, going against his sullen acceptance of the situation, but it is important to see that even though Jezebel is the one who comes up with the plan and carries it through, Ahab, her husband, is still the one responsible for the actions of his wife before God. You see when God pronounces judgment through the prophet, Elijah, this is what He says.

"Arise, go down to meet Ahab king of Israel, who lives in Samaria. There he is, in the vineyard of Naboth; where he has gone down to take possession of it. You shall speak to him, saying, 'Thus says the Lord: Have you murdered and also taken possession?' And you shall speak to him, saying, 'Thus says the Lord: In the place where dogs licked the blood of Naboth, dogs shall lick your blood, even yours.'" (I Kings 21:18-19)

God also goes on to declare that Ahab's posterity will be taken away, his lineage will die, and that "The dogs shall eat Jezebel by the wall of Jezreel." (1 Kings 21:23) In this example, please note that not only was Jezebel judged for totally disobeying God and overruling her husband, but Ahab also was held accountable for his wife's actions and judged. I don't know about you, but I don't think I want to be the one responsible for a harsh judgment on my husband because of something I did in overruling him.

If we skip over to the New Testament, in Acts 5: 1-11, we read about another couple, Ananias, and Sapphira, his wife.

"But a certain man named Ananias, with Sapphira his wife, sold a possession. And he kept back part of the proceeds, his wife also being aware of it, and brought a certain part and laid it at the apostles' feet. But Peter said, "Ananias, why has Satan filled your heart to lie to the Holy Spirit and keep back part of the price of the land for yourself? While it remained, was it not your own? And after it was sold, was it not in your own control? Why have you conceived this thing in your heart? You have not lied to men but to God." Then Ananias, hearing these words, fell down and breathed his last. So great fear came upon all those who heard these things. And the young men arose and wrapped him up, carried him out, and buried him. Now it was about three hours later when his wife came in, not knowing what had happened. And Peter answered her, "Tell me whether you sold the land for so much?" She said, "Yes, for so much." Then Peter said to her, "How is it that you have agreed together to test the Spirit of the Lord? Look, the feet of those who have buried your husband are at the door, and they will carry you out." Then immediately she fell down at his feet and breathed her last. And the young men came in and found her dead, and carrying her out, buried her by her husband. So great fear came upon all the church and upon all who heard these things."

Here, Sapphira clearly obeyed her husband by lying about the money. So why does God judge her for submitting to her husband? How was Abigail's defiance different from Sapphira's submission? How were Jezebel's efforts to please Ahab different from Sarah's efforts to obey Abraham?

The difference seems to be in their attitudes toward God. In Abigail's situation, she knew that her husband's decision was dishonoring to God with regard to the one He had anointed to be ruler over Israel. Her words in 1 Samuel 25: 26-31 confirm this when she says,

"For the LORD will certainly make for my lord an enduring house, because my lord fights the battles of the LORD, and evil is not found in you throughout your days… And it shall come to pass, when the LORD has done for my lord according to all the good that He has spoken concerning you, and has appointed you ruler over Israel, that this will be no grief to you, nor offense of heart to my lord…"

Abigail knew that David was the Lord's anointed ruler over Israel and that he fought the battles of the Lord, and that if she was to honor God, then she must honor David, a man in a position of God-given authority. Jezebel, a worshiper of Baal, hated God and seemed to delight in wickedness, as it says in 1 Kings 21:25-26,

> "But there was no one like Ahab who sold himself to do wickedness in the sight of the Lord, because Jezebel his wife stirred him up. And he behaved very abominably in following idols, according to all that the Amorites had done, whom the Lord has cast out before the children of Israel."

Sapphira, in Acts, did not seem to fully realize the severity of lying to God. She followed her husband without regard to the falseness of their action, which dishonored God and the church. Knowing these things, let's summarize the information in a chart so that we can clearly see what is involved in our decisions regarding our husbands.

In every situation, we have two choices to make. First, we can choose to honor God or to dishonor God, and second, we can choose to follow and submit to our husbands, or to follow our own plans. Putting the examples of these women in chart form, then would look like this:

Example:	Sarah	Abigail	Sapphira	Jezebel
Choice 1:	Honor God		Dishonor God	
Choice 2:	Follow husband	Overrule husband	Follow husband	Overrule husband
Results:	God protected	God rewarded	God killed	God judged

It seems, from the chart, that God protects, defends, honors, and rewards those who fear Him. It also seems that God judges those who fail to give Him the honor He is due. So, even though it sounds like I am suggesting that no matter what the situation is, you are to submit your husband, that is not true. The most important thing is to honor

God, to fear Him, to reverence Him. Once that proper attitude toward God is in place, then if your husband asks you to do something that is clearly outside God's commandments, then you will have a choice to make. Sarah chose to obey Abraham even when it put her in another man's harem, and God was able to protect her. Abigail chose to obey God and honor Him and His anointed, rather than submit to her husband and God rewarded her. Both women had crucial decisions to make, neither decision was taken lightly, but in the end, they both chose to honor God above all.

N THE MOST IMPORTANT THING IS TO HONOR GOD. *N*

Now I know that some of you reading this may be married to a man who has not believed that Jesus died for his sins and knows nothing of God, one who is not following God, or one who may actually resent your relationship with the Lord and the time and resources you spend on Him. That may make your decisions about honoring God or obeying your husband even more difficult. In fact, you may be very scared to submit yourself to an ungodly man. God talks about that in 1 Peter 3:1 when Peter writes,

> "Wives, likewise, be submissive to your own husbands,... that even if some do not obey the word, they, without a word, may be won by the conduct of their wives, when they observe your chaste conduct accompanied by fear."

Even if our husbands do not obey the word, and need to be won, we are still to fear, love, and trust God, to put aside our anger and resentment, to put on love for our husbands, to submit to them with a sweet attitude, respecting them and honoring their preferences in our actions and speech. Why? So that they may be won without a word by our conduct. Peter never says anything about preaching to them or leaving them tracts, or trying to manipulate them by agreeing to submit if they will obey the Word. It says we are only to speak with our conduct. If our conduct towards them changes because we have decided to trust and obey God, then they cannot help but see it.

Imagine your joy if your choice of submission with love and respect leads your husband, without a word, to God.

If you are in an abusive situation, I urge you to get godly counsel. If your husband asks you to do something that is clearly outside God's commandments, you will have a difficult choice to make. Sarah chose to obey Abraham even when it put her in another man's harem, and God was able to protect her. So also, He is able to take care of you, but there may be consequences. If you choose to obey God, rather than your husband, as Abigail did, you must be willing to respectfully and lovingly take the consequences of your non-submission to your husband from him. But even though we looked at the example of Abigail, who honored God but still overruled her husband, I don't want you to use her as an excuse not to submit to your husband if it is at all possible. Lack of submission to our husbands is a decision that should *never* be taken lightly nor without the counsel or protection of a higher authority, such as that of the church or the civil government.

If you are reading this and are not yet married, but have someone in mind as a potential candidate, please look carefully at your choice. Make sure now, that you can trust him and that you are willing to respect him and submit to him lovingly. Please don't be deceived into thinking that you can change him after you are married. Changing him doesn't work and is not your job. You won't get your own way.

The most important point I want you to see as we look at the example of God's working in the lives of Sarah and Abraham and as you look at your own life is this. It is so important. The point is: **that if we, as women, are faithful to follow our husbands in all their decisions, whether good or bad, God is big enough to take care of us.** You see, the issue is more than trusting our husbands, the issue is trusting God. **Do you truly believe that God is strong enough, wise enough, and willing enough to take care of you if you choose, from your heart, to obey Him by submitting to your husband?** This is a big question. It is a faith question, and one you will have to answer for yourself, before you will let God change you into the woman He wants you to be.

DO YOU BELIEVE THAT GOD IS STRONG ENOUGH, WISE ENOUGH AND WILLING ENOUGH TO TAKE CARE OF YOU IF YOU CHOOSE TO SUBMIT TO YOUR HUSBAND?

Further Study for Chapter 13:

David was a "man after God's own heart" and trusted God completely. Read Psalm 4, 16, 84 and 125, and reflect on God's trustworthiness.

CHAPTER 14:

Letting the Leader Lead
a.k.a. Respectful Following

OK. Now that you have gotten rid of your resentment and have decided to trust God and submit to your husband, what do you do? How do you live? If you have been leading, how do you quit? How do you encourage your husband to lead? What if you don't think your husband is capable of leading? Take a look at this next verse. What does it tell us to do?

> (Ephesians 5:33) "Nevertheless let each one of you in particular so love his own wife as himself, and let the wife see that she respects her husband."

As women, we want to be loved; we need to feel loved. Women want to be loved unconditionally, not for what we do, but for who we are. So God tells our husbands to love us.

For our husbands, they want to be significant; they need to feel respected. If they don't feel respected, they won't feel loved. Men want to be affirmed unconditionally, not for how well they lead, or how well they do, but just for who they are. So God tells us to respect our husbands.

↷ OUR HUSBANDS WANT TO BE AFFIRMED AND RESPECTED UNCONDITIONALLY. *↷*

This doesn't seem that complicated. If we look at what God created, we see that He is the one who created the two sexes. He created male and female in His image to complement each other. If God had wanted to put all of His qualities into Adam, there would have been no need for Eve. But God is too complex and immense and wonderful to cram into just one sex, so he made male and female to make His image complete in the marriage relationship. God is all-powerful, all-knowing, all-protecting, all-providing, worthy of fear and awe and reverence. He created men to reflect this side of His nature. God is also very tender, nurturing, and loving, caring for His children as a nursing mother with her babies. He created women to reflect this side of His nature. When we confuse the roles of men and women, with each sex trying to take on the role of the other, it causes confusion and unhappiness in our lives and in our marriages as neither sex achieves what God had really planned. Neither sex is able to complement and enhance the other for the maximum good, and the image of God is distorted because of the world's lies about the roles of men and women.

Satan has put into place a system of thinking about leadership that "unmans" our men and promotes leadership in the wrong places. If you were to ask, most people would say they want good leaders in government and in the workplace. In the name of equal opportunity, some countries try to promote women as leaders in the workplace. In the United States, for example, presidents who appoint women to high positions in government are hailed as forward thinkers and supportive of women's rights. Now I'm not saying that women can't be effective leaders, but biologically, God designed men to be better analysts and decision makers, and He designed women to be better nurturers, so when we as a society applaud women in leadership, we are actually applauding a system which diminishes the respect for male leadership and encourages women to have to work harder to achieve good results. This warped thinking can also carry over into our families. Just as women are encouraged to lead in the workplace, and want to lead because of the judgment, so also they are encouraged to lead at home, trapping the men who want to lead their families into the untenable situation of being called chauvinistic and harsh. Any man who wants to lead, must somehow gain power over the woman who is already leading. Unfortunately, if the woman is not willing to give up her power, he faces the dilemma of how to gain power without being accused of bullying her, and discrediting him and his leadership. Most men in that situation, will simply step out of the leadership role and look for other places where they can lead in order to be respected and affirmed.

So, why is this important? Because if you, as a wife have been leading in your home or have been contemptuous of your husband's leading, whether knowingly or not, then your husband is probably feeling frustrated and disrespected. In that situation, he may look for respect somewhere else. It may be in the workplace where his working long hours is noted and rewarded, or at the church or in a community organization working with people who will see and appreciate his efforts. He may choose to get involved in pornography, where the images of women offer him easy, counterfeit intimacy, false respect and fake affirmation, or he may choose to invest himself in an affair, whether emotional or physical, where the "other woman" gives him the approval he craves at home. He could choose to bury his disappointment in alcohol, drugs, gambling or some other addictive behavior. We, as wives, are not ultimately responsible for the choices that our men make, but when we disregard the instructions that God has given us concerning our respectful treatment and affirmation of them, then we can unwittingly nudge them into paths that lead to unhealthy lives and marriages.

When my marriage was at its lowest point, I felt like my husband was having an affair. Not with another woman, but with the church. He spent his time and energy serving there, while I felt rejected and betrayed at home. I had fallen into a vicious cycle of disrespect. I was angry and bitter about many things; I questioned his leadership and didn't succeed at hiding my bad attitude toward him. He was not getting the respect and affirmation he needed at home, so he volunteered at the church where he was hailed as a great guy. The more he volunteered, the more resentful I became, the more he volunteered, and so on. Our marriage couldn't improve until I dealt with my anger and chose to respect and affirm my husband at home, so that he would then want to be home with me rather than spending excessive hours volunteering at the church. My ignorance of the importance of respecting my husband and his leadership was very damaging to our marriage. That is why God tells us in Ephesians to respect our husbands.

🖊 **RESPECT FOR OUR HUSBANDS AND THEIR LEADERSHIP IS CRITICAL TO A GOOD MARRIAGE.** 🖊

So, now that we know how important it is, how do we respect our husbands and encourage them to lead? Well, once again, I can share my story, and maybe we can find some principles that will work for you.

When I first realized that I was fallible, that I could make mistakes, and that my husband could be right, I began to see my need of seeking his advice and help, i.e. leadership, not only in big issues, but also in small ones. I learned that if I asked for his advice, I had to be willing to follow it. I found that if I wasn't willing to follow his advice, or if I wanted to argue about it, then it was best not to ask him for it, for by rejecting his advice, ignoring it or arguing about it, I was being disrespectful.

I learned that a good place to start asking his advice was with the issues that caused me to get angry with him in the first place. In my case, it was the garbage. When we were first married, it was John's job to take out the garbage. By the time we had one small child, and I was no longer working outside the home, I found that I was home with the trash can every day, all day. The garbage became a sore point in my life because John did not take it out very regularly. I felt like I should do it since I was home all day, but he had said that it was his job. He didn't take it out when I expected him to, so I would get mad, (an unmet expectation) and disrespect him in my heart. I didn't want to nag, so I seethed quietly. I would finally get tired of the overflowing trash can and so I would take it out myself feeling very self-righteous for having performed a good deed, just for my husband, who obviously needed my help. I also resented John because I should not have had to do that good deed in the first place. I struggled with my resentment until I decided to ask his advice. He declared that it was his job and that he would do it. That was very freeing for me to have clear directions on what to do, or in this case, not to do, about the garbage. I didn't take it out any more after that. He still did not take it out very regularly, and it still overflowed, but my attitude had changed. Now, as I passed the overflowing can, I would say to myself, *"It is not my job. John has asked me not to take it out, and I can respect his wishes and rest knowing that he will take care of it."* When I found myself getting frustrated about it, I would pray,

"God, you know about this garbage. You know that John has said I am not to take it out. I am going to obey him, respectfully, in what he has asked me to do, and I am going to trust you to motivate him to do what he said he would do. Please take my frustration, and help me to trust him and You. Amen."

I want you to notice that nothing about the situation had changed except my attitude.

> ↯ WE CANNOT ALWAYS CHANGE
> THE SITUATION,
> BUT WE CAN ALWAYS CHANGE
> OUR ATTITUDE. ↯

Fortunately or unfortunately, about that time, my parents came for a visit. Now my dad is a take charge kind of person and likes everything in order. He could not understand why I didn't just take out the garbage and why I wouldn't let him take it out. I said I wouldn't, because it wasn't my job and he shouldn't, because it wasn't his job. I know he was confused, but it was a big step for me to be able to rest in obedience to my husband's decision, even in the face of my dad's confusion. Eventually, John started taking out the garbage more regularly, and the most wonderful thing about it was that I never had to say a word, make a remark or worry about it. I left his job in his hands and he stepped up and took charge.

So, what are the possible principles about respecting our husbands in this oh-so-trivial event in my life.

🖊 Discuss clearly and calmly, the issue that is causing a problem for you with your husband. Let him know, as completely as you can, what you are thinking and feeling, laying it all before him. If you don't feel like you can be calm and respectful during a discussion, then you might want to write down your thoughts and concerns. Let him read them without an emotional torrent. Your discussion can continue from there. If your husband is in a situation where he is extremely busy, and may not have time for a long discussion at that moment, then you might write your concerns and give them to him to read when he has time to consider them thoroughly. I know that when I write letters to John and leave them for him, he appreciates the opportunity to read them when he knows he can concentrate on what I have written.

🖊 Let your husband give you clear instructions on what he wants to do about the problem.

🖊 Follow his instructions, respectfully accepting his decision, **whether or not you agree.**

🖊 Ask God to help you to obey and to take care of any bad attitudes you might develop, even if the situation does not change. Remember you *can* change the way you choose to respond.

🖊 Rest in your husband's decision and don't take it over again. Do not fret or worry about it, realizing that God will hold *him* accountable for the decision, and that God will hold you accountable for your response.

Now I know that some of you may be thinking, *"But my problem is so much bigger than a garbage can,"* and you are probably right. What about the husband who wants to be responsible for the household bills? He has asked his wife to put them in a certain spot, so that he can be responsible for paying them. Unfortunately, he forgets about them, and doesn't end up paying them on time. Is it right in that case for the wife to take the initiative and pay them? Absolutely not, because he has not delegated that authority to her. Her job is to put them where he asked her to put them. If the electricity is cut off, then it is her job to cheerfully serve him a cold, candlelight supper. **When our husbands realize that we are no longer going to take over and usurp their authority, then they will have greater freedom to step up and take charge.** Allowing our husbands to fail and letting God work in their hearts without interference from us helps them to grow into the leaders God designed them to be. It may be a painful, expensive process as our husbands learn to lead, but it is one which they must experience if they are to develop. Unfortunately, if you choose to step out of the leadership role in your marriage, and begin to follow your husband, there are no guarantees that he will begin to lead and no guarantees that your marriage will improve. But God asks us to follow Him and to do what He says. If we choose to follow God and submit to our husband, respecting and affirming him, despite the results, we are pleasing God and will receive our reward one day in heaven. Remember, with God's help, the only person we can change is our self. God is going to have to change our husbands. We just interfere when we keep getting in the way.

∿ ALLOWING OUR HUSBANDS TO FAIL
SO THAT GOD CAN WORK IN THEM WITHOUT OUR INTERFERENCE
HELPS THEM TO GROW INTO THE LEADERS
GOD DESIGNED THEM TO BE. *∿*

In closing, I want to give you a word of hope. I know my husband may just be incredibly exceptional, but it didn't take long for John to start leading once he knew I would follow. Once I moved out of the way, trusted God and welcomed John's leadership, respecting him and his decisions, I found that he quickly developed into a great leader. The unexpected bonus was the freedom I felt. When I was finally willing to trust God and my husband, I learned that my husband was capable, wise and able to take care of me. The frustration and uncertainty of trying to make all the decisions and trying to always be right was replaced by the freedom of resting in the care of a wonderful man and an awesome God.

Further Study for Chapter 14:

Read Luke 6:46-49.

What 3 things did the man in verse 47 do?

What happened when the flood came?

What did the man in verse 49 do?

What happened when the flood came?

Read Luke 8:21.

Who are Jesus' mother and brothers?

Read Luke 11:28

Who are those who are blessed?

Read 1 John 5:1-5

Who are those who love the children of God?

Are His commandments hard?

We are fighting Satan's world system. What will overcome it?

Through our faith, we can overcome the world. God tells us that those who love Him and are blessed, are those who *hear* His word and commandments and actually *do* them, stepping out in faith. God tells us to respect, submit to, and follow our husbands. We have heard His word. The real question is:

Will we obey Him?

Isaiah 32:17 says,

"The work of righteousness will be peace, and the effect of righteousness, quietness and assurance forever."

 WOULDN'T IT BE LOVELY TO BE AT PEACE, QUIET AND ASSURED BECAUSE WE HAVE OBEYED GOD BY RESPECTING AND FOLLOWING OUR HUSBANDS?

CHAPTER 15:
What's Next? Priorities

(Genesis 2:18) "And the Lord God said, 'It is not good that man should be alone; I will make him a helper comparable to him.'"

For those of you who like to be buzzing around, constantly doing things, this may be a hard chapter. This is a chapter on "being." In Genesis, God says that it is not good that man should be alone, so He makes woman, a helper for him. That would suggest then, that we wives are to be with our husbands so that they are not alone. Since I am one of those women who is nearly constantly in motion, with a long list of To-Do items, I can commiserate with those of you who feel compelled to have the house spotless, the church committees running well, and the rest of life organized and taken care of. But I've talked to a number of wives who spend so much time on their activities that their husbands get "left alone." One woman had experienced the bad effects of her parent's divorce when she was young, and vowed that she would never divorce. She also vowed never to let herself be vulnerable, and to be hurt like her mother, so she refused to trust her husband. Since she had to prepare for her own support, in case he divorced her, she spent long hours going to school and working, rather than spending time with him. She later admitted to me that in their three-story house, every one had their own floor. She had one, her husband had one, and their only child had one. Because of her lack of trust that God would take care of her if she let herself be dependent on her husband, she trapped herself and her husband into miserable lonely existences. It is not good.

That is not the only way in which we can leave our husbands alone. We can do it with the best of intentions. One woman has a job in which she cares for other people. Her husband seems to support the idea of her working. She truly loves helping these people, and would like to take on more responsibility for caring for others, but she admits that she gets up early, goes to work, gets back late and goes to bed long before her husband, and doesn't see how this additional care would fit in. What she hasn't seen is that her husband probably needs extra care too, since he is often alone, and she hasn't realized that maybe her husband needs to become a priority.

What about the woman who doesn't want to work, but has to, perhaps because her husband is incapacitated, in school, in training, or is in the midst of setting up his own business, so that he can take care of her later. Not only does she have to work, but she might also feel compelled to take perfect care of the house. Every dish must be done, every article out of place must be straightened, and every pillow must be fluffed. But there are only so many hours in the day. If she is a good steward of her job and her house, she can't spend time with her husband. Her husband, on the other hand, just wants her beside him. He doesn't care if the dishes are stacked up, or the laundry sits unfolded in the basket, he just wants her to be with him. I know how difficult it is to sit in the same room with your husband and just be there, when your mind is spinning with all the things that need to be done. But those things will always need to be done, and your husband needs not to be alone. Let's look at a passage from Luke 10:38-42.

> "Now it happened as they went that He entered a certain village; and a certain woman named Martha welcomed Him into her house. And she had a sister called Mary, who also sat at Jesus' feet and heard His word. But Martha was distracted with much serving, and she approached Him and said, 'Lord, do You not care that my sister has left me to serve alone? Therefore tell her to help me.' And Jesus answered and said to her, 'Martha, Martha, you are worried and troubled about many things. But one thing is needed, and Mary has chosen that good part, which will not be taken away from her.'"

Titus 2:4 tells the older women to "...admonish the young women to love their husbands, ..." How can we love them? ...by not leaving them alone, by choosing the good part of sitting at their feet or beside them on the couch. Yes, I know that there are things which need to be done in order to be a good *housewife*, but we need to find a balance between the many things, and the one thing of being a good *wife* to our husband. How do we do that? Start by remembering that your husband is the leader. A leader's job is to figure out a plan, a strategy so that all the things that need to be done will get done. So, ask the leader. Since most men love solving problems, what better way is there to show love toward them than to let them solve ours? When we follow their advice, not only does it make them feel respected, valued and loved, but we also are blessed by being able to spend our energy doing those things which we have been asked to do, without fretting and stewing over what we think is the best thing to do.

In the early stages of my decision to live as a changed wife, I would ask John what he would like me to do that day. That may seem like overkill, but I had just realized how utterly wrong my daily decisions had been, and I wanted to be sure I started out right. For me, it was the best way. John was very patient with me as he gave me instructions, and at the end of the day, I found joy in knowing that I had followed him with a full heart. Even now, when I seem to have too many things to do, I will come to John and lay my schedule before him. I will tell him what has already been planned, repeat to him the thing that he has asked me to do, and then simply say, "I can't do all of this. What would you like me to cut, or how can I make this all work? Where do you want me to find the time you need for me to spend with you?" Consistently, he has been understanding and supportive of my problems and often comes up with a very creative solutions (ones that I would never have thought of) to solve them. I have found his leadership abilities to be helpful in other areas as well, not just scheduling.

Now you may feel like you have things more under control than I did, and you may not need to take the very drastic step of asking your husband what he wants or needs done. You may feel that asking for his advice is just one more burden for him to have to shoulder, especially if you know that he is overwhelmed with things at work or church or wherever else his energies are required. But since God has made him the head of the household, it is alright for you to ask for his leadership. It is his job. It is a way to show him the respect that we are commanded to give to him. He also may really appreciate the opportunity for directing your activities so that the things that you do actually help both of you.

Consider this trivial example. Suppose you have your own schedule under control, and suppose your husband asks you to pick up his shirts at the cleaners during the course of your day. Suppose you have time to complete every other errand except for picking up his shirts. When he gets home and asks where they are you have to respond with an, "Oops, I forgot, I'm sorry," or an excuse, "Well, you know this and that and the other thing came up and I just didn't get around to it." If you were your husband, how would you feel at this point? Would you feel valuable, respected, important and loved or would you feel like you were less important than everything else? Your husband probably really needed those shirts, and instead of helping him, you have actually created more work for him as he has to figure out something else to wear to that big meeting tomorrow. He probably would rather have had you tell him that your day was already full, and that you needed his help to sort things out, rather than end up in a mini-crisis. The few minutes he would have spent with you in sorting out the priorities of things that needed to be done that day would probably have been much less than the many minutes required to figure out an alternative. Our reluctance to ask our husbands to lead can actually hinder them rather than help them. It is so freeing to realize that we don't have to do everything our own way. Just as God gave Eve to Adam to be a helper suitable for him, He gave Eve a leader to save her from her own deceived way. What better way to show love towards our husbands than by letting them lead and making their needs and requests a priority.

> *Our reluctance to ask our husbands to lead can actually hinder them rather than help them.* *

In the eyes of the world, it is foolish and weak to serve your husband in love, making his needs a priority, letting him set agendas, and schedules, and putting aside time to be just with him without other distractions. Satan and his world system would say we should make ourselves like the Most High, having our own way, asserting ourselves over others, obeying our own ideas and not subjecting ourselves to any man. But the wisdom of the world is foolishness to the Lord, and God is able to use the foolish and weak things of the world to shame those who are wise and strong. (1 Corinthians 1:18-31) What freedom, strength, and joy we receive we turn away from the world's system, submit ourselves to God and do things His way!

Further Study for Chapter 15:

Read 1 Timothy 2:8-15.

According to verse 10, with what are godly women
to adorn themselves?

When we nag, tell our husbands what to do, set their schedules or
demand things of them, are we abiding by verses 11 and 12?

In verses 13 and 14, what 2 reasons does God give for women to submit
to man's authority?

Does verse 15 make sense?

    The Nelson Study Bible gives an explanation and says,
"The salvation referred to here is not justification, but daily sanctification.
Most likely, Paul is referring to being delivered from the desire to dominate
by recognizing one's appropriate place in God's creation order."[1]

---

[1]   The Nelson Study Bible, pp. 2044-2045, Thomas Nelson, Inc., 1997

CHAPTER 16:
Is That All?
The List of To-Dos

For those of you who love lists and love to check them off, these next two sets of verses are for you. They contain "to-do" lists; those things which we can do to and for our husbands to be the godly wives God intended us to be.

We've already covered 1 Peter 3:1-2,

"Wives, likewise, be submissive to your own husbands, ...that even if some do not obey the word, they, without a word, may be won by the conduct of their wives, when they observe your chaste conduct accompanied by fear,"

but what about 1 Peter 3:3-4?

"Do not let your adornment be merely outward--arranging the hair, wearing gold, or putting on fine apparel--rather let it be the hidden person of the heart, with the incorruptible beauty of a gentle and quiet spirit, which is very precious in the sight of God."

Here, God doesn't tell us to be a slob or not care about our outward appearance. God designed men to be visual creatures, and so our appearance is important to them. An attractive wife at home can help our husbands to avoid temptation from other attractive women in the workplace. In addition, many men judge other men and feel judged by other men on the appearance of their wives. If a man has a well-groomed, confident woman by his side, then other men assume that that man is successful in all areas of his life. If a man is married to a woman who obviously takes no pains to keep herself attractive, then other men will feel sorry for him, and will think that they can get the best of him in their next business deal. When we, as wives, do not make the effort to keep our outward appearance attractive for our husbands, then they feel pitied and disrespected by other men, and unloved by us. In Ephesians 5:25-29 it says,

"Husbands, love your wives, just as Christ also loved the church and gave Himself for her, that He might sanctify and cleanse her with the washing of water by the word, that He might present her to Himself a glorious church, not having spot or wrinkle or any such thing, but that she should be holy and without blemish. So husbands ought to love their own wives as their own bodies; he who loves his wife loves himself. For no one ever hated his own flesh, but nourishes and cherishes it, just as the Lord does the church."

Our husbands are to love us as Christ loved the church. Just as Christ nourishes and cherishes the church in order to present her to Himself as a glorious church without spot or wrinkle, so our husbands should want to take care of us and to nourish us so that we are presented to them as glorious wives. Our husbands are to love us as they love their own bodies, so just as they make an effort to keep themselves clean and fit, so also, they desire us to be clean and fit. When we neglect ourselves and our outward appearance, our husbands may see it as a reflection on them and their ability to take care of all things. Therefore, it is wise for us to take care of ourselves and to present ourselves in a pleasing and charming manner for our husbands. But, God also tells us that the outward appearance is not the *only* thing. The hidden person of the heart is also important. I have heard more than one man say that although physical beauty is immediately appealing to the eye, when it is accompanied by a haughty, spiteful, mean spirit, it loses all its appeal. God sees as "very precious" a gentle and quiet spirit. It is impossible to be gentle or quiet if your heart is full of anger or disgust. If we will work on letting God have His way with our inner self, to break it, cleanse it, and refashion it according to His design, then our beauty will be incorruptible and never fade, and our husbands cannot help but see it and be influenced by it.

1 Peter 3:5-6 it continues with,

"For in this manner, in former times, the holy women who trusted in God also adorned themselves, being submissive to their own husbands, as Sarah obeyed Abraham, calling him lord, whose daughters you are if you do good and are not afraid with any terror."

Holy women, in times past, have adorned themselves with this gentle and quiet spirit, born of a trust in God and His care and provision for them, in spite of what their husbands might choose to do. Sarah obeyed Abraham, calling him lord, not being afraid with any terror, even when her obedience would take her out of Abraham's household and care. The only way she could have submitted to Abraham's commands without being afraid was by trusting God. She must have known that God was big enough, strong enough and powerful enough to take care of her in spite of Abraham.

Titus 2:4-5 has a list of what "young women" are to learn:

"...to love their husbands, to love their children, to be discreet, chaste, homemakers, good, obedient to their own husbands, that the word of God may not be blasphemed."

We've already dealt with loving our husbands by getting rid of our resentment and putting on love, and by respecting them and seeking their leadership. There are two more important ways to show love to our husbands. Earlier, we touched on one of them, about not leaving our husbands alone. We discussed the importance of letting them schedule our time so that we have time to spend with them. That time with them does not necessarily have to be spent beside them on the couch, but could include other things such as: taking a walk with them, discussing something you have both read, going to the store with them, or sitting and watching them fix something around the house. My mother used to sit for hours on a step watching my father fix our car. She couldn't help him, except to pass him the occasional tool, and she wasn't all that interested in the mechanics of the car, but she knew that it was *important to him* for her to be there with him. Our husbands feel loved and respected when we spend time with them and an important part of loving them is choosing to put aside our own plans in order to do that.

For our husbands, the perfect ending to spending time with their wives is sex. For them, sex is not always a "stand alone" event, but rather, the physical act of making love completes the emotional closeness that was begun by doing something together. Making love makes our husbands feel powerful, attractive and desirable, but there is a big difference between *allowing* your husband to love you in the bedroom, and enthusiastically participating *with him* in the bedroom. Often, we women aren't always quick to want to make love, especially if it has been a long day with work, the kids or housework. But if we will take a few moments to mentally prepare ourselves for intimate time with our husbands, while we are spending time with them, or cooking, or before they come home from work, then we will be ready to welcome them with open arms and enjoy the physical act of love that God created for our marriages. When physical love is lacking in a marriage, so too is emotional closeness between the man and his wife.

Sex is important not only to the health of our marriages, but also to the physical and emotional health of our men. If our men feel rejected or inadequate in the bedroom, then they can also feel inadequate and discouraged as they go about their jobs and lives. But when our husbands feel like big, strong heroes in the bedroom, then they are more likely to feel like big, strong heroes in all other areas of life. We, as wives, have an incredible ability to send our men out into the world each day, vigorous and encouraged, because they know that they are strong and virile in the eyes of their wives. Loving our husbands includes putting aside bad attitudes toward them, respecting them, allowing them to lead, choosing to spend time with them, and enthusiastically making love to them.

The next part of Titus 2:4 tells us to love our children, but since this dissertation is not about how to deal with our children, we must be to the part that talks about being discreet. What does that mean? Well, to be discreet means to be sound in mind, wise, politic, considerate. It generally refers to our speech. There are two ways in which we, as women, are to consider our speech in regard to our men. The first is to be wise in the words that we use when we communicate with them to their faces and the second is to be wise in the words that we use about them in public. One thing to remember when we talk with our husbands face-to-face is that in spite of their manly demeanor, the words and mannerisms that we use can easily wound them. Anytime that we, as women, talk to them in such a way that they feel subordinate, challenged or that they feel like we do not trust them, they may feel threatened and unloved. Each one of you will need to figure out what tones, words or expressions hurt your particular man. I know for many men, the use of *not* or the contraction *n't* at the beginning of a question is often seen as a challenge to their authority. For example, if you say to a man, "Haven't you taken the garbage out yet?" or, "Why didn't you take out the garbage?", they may feel insulted and think that you are really saying that you don't trust them to take care of the garbage, that you don't think they're capable of taking the garbage out, or that you don't believe that they have a plan for taking care of the garbage. I have found that for my husband, a better way to ask is to say, "Have you taken out the garbage?" or "When are you planning to take out the garbage?" Because I haven't posed the question as a challenge, then my husband believes that I just want an update on his plans for the garbage.

Another area in which we need to be wise in our speech to our husbands is when we offer to help them. They like to do things their way, and they want us to be proud of them for doing it well. When we say things like, "Let me help you." or "It would be better if you <u>(fill in the blank)</u> ", then our husbands might construe our words as, "She doesn't think I know what I'm doing, she doesn't trust me to take care of things, or she thinks she can do it better." All of these interpretations make our men feel disrespected and unloved. In our house, I have found that I need to say, "Is there anything I can do to help?" or "Do you want my help?" Then my husband feels like I trust his plan and know that he has everything under control, and is free to accept or reject my offer of help as necessary.

I know that these suggestions may seem small, petty and unimportant, but they aren't. In the early years of my marriage I did not understand the importance of communicating discreetly with my husband, and many of my questions and offers of help, phrased with negative contractions and unsolicited advice, were seen as challenges to his competency and ego. He will admit that those first few years of your marriage were some of the most miserable of his life, and it was due in large part to how I spoke to him and to my use of challenging language. Even though these seem like small changes to make, being wise in the small things as well as in the large can make huge differences to the way our husbands feel that we are treating them, and in turn, can improve our marriages.

The other part of being discreet in our speech has to do with how we speak about our husbands in public. How do you speak about your husband either in front of him or behind his back? Does he see that you praise him and build him up in front of others, or does he know that you criticize and show disregard for him in your conversations. Throughout Proverbs and James, God tells us to be wise, restrained and sagacious in our conversation. In Matthew 15:18, Jesus says, "But those things which proceed out of the mouth come from the heart, and they defile a man." As we consider our speech with others, we must be aware of what we really think about our husbands in our hearts. If the image we carry is unloving, weak and hateful, then those thoughts and images will spew out of our mouths. If, however, we have dealt with our resentment and disrespect towards him, then things of good report will issue from our mouths concerning him. Essentially, if our thinking about our husband has changed, then it should show up in our actions and words. It is very important for our husbands to know that their reputation and image are safe in our hands. If we continually discredit them before the world, they will know it and there can be no change in our marriages. The new you must show not only in your changed actions and attitudes, but also in your speech.

The Titus 2 list continues with being chaste. What does it mean to be chaste? To be pure and undefiled. Purity is a characteristic that involves the whole person or whole thing. If you make a pure sauce and add moldy cheese, the whole sauce is no longer pure. It has been defiled. So too, if we have decided to fear and revere the Lord in some things, but not in all, then the whole person is defiled. But what are some of the things that can defile us? Gossip, dwelling on the sordid affairs of others, lying to our husbands about what we do with our time or our money, getting emotionally involved with other men, harboring grudges, etc. The list can be long. We need to realize that chasteness is a purity of the whole person, body, mind and soul. It starts with being clean before the Lord. We must examine our hearts and confess our sin, pride and poor attitudes to the Lord. He has promised that "If we confess our sins, He is faithful and just to forgive us our sins and to cleanse us from all unrighteousness." (1 John 1:9) Once the Lord has cleansed us, then we are free to be chaste and undefiled as we walk with our husbands in love.

Titus also tells us to be homemakers. What is a homemaker? To have as our primary occupation, the making and keeping of the home. My favorite definition of homemaking is found in The Book of Knowledge. It says,

"Homemaking is the most important job in the world. Whether the home is a house or an apartment, whether it is in a city or a village or on a farm, it is the unit on which civilization is built. For a home is not just a place, but a place plus people--a family. Thus all the activities of civilization revolve around the home; agriculture, industry, commerce and transportation; art and science, medicine and research; education and religion... The word 'homemaker' means a person who not only cares for the house but does so with the love, tact and understanding of human relationships that turn a house into a happy home.... The aim and greatest reward of real homemaking is a

happy and healthy family. "[2]

Proverbs 31 talks about the virtuous wife. Her occupations were primarily concerned with watching over the ways of her household by providing food for her household, weaving, making clothing, decorating her home. She also helped the poor, bought and sold property and sold merchandise which she had made. She did these things to help her husband so that he would "have no lack of gain. She does him good and not evil all the days of her life." (Proverbs 31:11b-12)

These verses do not in any way prohibit a woman from working outside the home, but they do suggest that the emphasis for a wife is to work for the benefit of her husband by taking care of the home. If your husband desires that you work outside the home and both of you are satisfied with the way that the jobs are done and the home is taken care of, then you are right where you need to be. But if your husband would prefer that you be at home rather than having a career, then please hear him, consider his words, pray about the situation, consider giving up your job, and perhaps lowering your standard of living so that you can submit to him. Be content with what you have, trust God to supply your needs, and become a keeper of the home. If you are currently working, but truly desire to be at home, talk with your husband, discuss possibilities of lowering your expenditures so that you could stay home. Lay your desires before him, and then abide by his decision, willingly and with a full heart. If you are considering marriage, this matter of staying home is a big issue. Please discuss it with your intended spouse before you say those final wedding vows. If he is counting on you to have a career and you are assuming that you will be staying home as a homemaker or if he is counting on you being home and you want to further your career, then you need to talk. This is more than just a decision about a job. This is a decision about how

---

[2]   The Grolier Society Inc. The Book of Knowledge. Volume 8, pp. 2881-2882. May 1956 printing.

you will live your whole life. Please be sure that you and your future spouse are striving for the same goal before you ever say, "I do."

The Titus 2 list goes on with being good and obedient to our husbands. We can do that when we are right before God and submitting to our husbands. But there is a last point in these verses that is often overlooked. God tells the older women to teach the younger women all these things so that "the word of God may not be blasphemed." To blaspheme means to revile, to speak evilly of, to defame. When we follow God's plan for our lives as women and wives, other people will see our example and God's Word may be honored and seen as valuable before them. But when we choose to live contrary to what God has said, following our own way, then others will see the discrepancy and may discredit, abuse or make fun of God or His Word because of what they see in us. I do not want to have to stand before God one day and have to explain why I allowed His Word to be blasphemed because I was a proud and rebellious wife. How much better it would be to allow God to change me so that I might hear, "Well done, good and faithful servant." (Matthew 25:23)

Further Study for Chapter 16:

Read Proverbs 31:10-31. These words are written by the mother of King Lemuel, so that he would know what to look for in a wife.

When you consider the words of verses 11 and 12, do you desire to be this kind of wife?

In verse 23, would her husband sit in the gates as an elder if she had not encouraged him to lead?

In verse 25, what is her clothing made of?

In verse 26, what comes out of her mouth?

In verse 27, how does she spend her days?

In verse 28, who praises her?

More importantly, why is she praised?

 OH, TO BE A WOMAN
WHO FEARS THE LORD!

CHAPTER 17:
Are You Weary?
Consider Jesus

I know that at this point you may be feeling a little overwhelmed. There is so much to think about, so much to do, so much to change. How can we possibly go on? We can go on because there is One who has gone on before us: Jesus. Take a few minutes to consider Jesus. Consider His person, His words, and His accomplishments. We are called to be good wives "likewise" or in the same manner as Jesus. If He is to be our example, then we need to consider Him, to reflect on Him. Fix yourself a nice cup of tea or coffee, find a really comfortable chair and just rest in and meditate on the following verses.

Are you discouraged by how much you have to learn and change and how hard it all seems?

> (Matthew 11:28-30) "Come to Me, all you who labor and are heavy laden, and I will give you rest. Take My yoke upon you and learn from Me, for I am gentle and lowly in heart, and you will find rest for your souls. For My yoke is easy and My burden is light."

Are you tired of trying to serve your husband and your family in love? Do you feel like you are the only one who is making an effort? Do you just wish that someone else would serve you for a change?

> (Matthew 20:26-28) "Yet it shall not be so among you; but whoever desires to become great among you, let him be your servant. And whoever desires to become first among you, let him be your slave--just as the Son of Man did not come to be served, but to serve, and to give His life a ransom for many."

> (John 13:14-15) "If I then, your Lord and Teacher, have washed your feet, you also ought to wash one another's feet. For I have given you an example, that you should do as I have done to you."

(John 13:34) "A new commandment I give to you, that you love one another; as I have loved you, that you also love one another."

(Romans 15:2-3a) "Let each of us please his neighbor for his good, leading to edification. For even Christ did not please himself..."

(2 Corinthians 8:9) "For you know the grace of our Lord Jesus Christ, that though he was rich, yet for your sakes He became poor, that you through His poverty might become rich."

(1 John 3:16) "By this we know love, because He laid down His life for us. And we also ought to lay down our lives for the brethren."

Do you find it hard to obey willingly? Do you still want your own way? Is pride still a problem?

(Philippians 2:5-8) "Let this mind be in you which was also in Christ Jesus, who, being in the form of God, did not consider it robbery to be equal with God, but made Himself of no reputation, taking the form of a bondservant, and coming in the likeness of men. And being found in appearance as a man, He humbled Himself and became obedient to the point of death, even the death of the cross."

(Colossians 3:9-11) "...you have put off the old man with his deeds, and have put on the new man who is renewed in knowledge according to the image of Him who created him, where ...Christ is all and in all."

Do you wonder how to walk or how to live?

(Ephesians 5:1-2) "Therefore be imitators of God as dear children. And walk in love, as Christ also has loved us and given Himself for us, an offering and a sacrifice to God for a sweet-smelling aroma."

(1 John 2:6) "He who says he abides in Him ought to walk just as He walked."

Are you afraid of what will happen if you put your old self aside and follow God's ways?

> (1 John 4:17-19) "Love has been perfected among us in this; that we may have boldness in the day of judgment; because as He is, so are we in this world. There is no fear in love; but perfect love casts out fear, because fear involves torment. But he who fears has not been made perfect in love. We love Him because He first loved us."

There is only one way to follow Jesus' example and that is to look to Him and consider Him.

> (Hebrews 12:1b-4) "...let us lay aside every weight, and the sin which so easily ensnares us, and let us run with endurance the race that is set before us, looking unto Jesus, the author and finisher of our faith, who for the joy that was set before Him endured the cross, despising the shame, and has sat down at the right hand of the throne of God. For consider Him who endured such hostility from sinners against Himself, lest you become weary and discouraged in your souls. You have not yet resisted to bloodshed, striving against sin."

> (Hebrews 3:1-2a) "Therefore, holy brethren, partakers of the heavenly calling, consider the Apostle and High Priest of our confession, Christ Jesus, who was faithful to Him who appointed Him..."

According to the world's system, set up by Satan, who wants his own way more than anything, we are to push for our own way, cater to our own pride, trust only in ourselves, rule over our husbands and ultimately destroy our marriages distorting the image of God to the world. But when we consider Jesus and His example, we can learn to trust God, to submit to our husbands, to lay aside our pride, our self-trust, our desire to rule and our bitterness, benefiting our marriages and living abundant lives as ambassadors for Christ.

We have a clear choice:

GOD'S WAY = FORGIVENESS, LOVE AND SUBMISSION.

OR

SATAN'S WAY = OUR WAY.

This is a faith decision. Will you consider Jesus, choose to trust God and follow His way, which means giving up your control and following your husband, or will you choose to follow the world's system that keeps control safely grasped within your own hands? Do you truly believe that God is big enough and strong enough to take care of you if you give control to your husband? Are you willing to let go of your former resentment and distrust of your husband? Are you willing to let God change *you*? If so, He *can* change your marriage for the better.

N IF YOU ARE WILLING
TO LET GOD CHANGE YOU,
HE CAN CHANGE YOUR MARRIAGE
FOR THE BETTER. *N*

Afterword

--by John Chapman, the husband of the author

I wanted to take a moment and write my thoughts as the guy who is in the background of the book you have just read. After all, I am the guy who didn't take out the trash.

First, to you ladies who have read my wife's book. I want to start out by disagreeing with something she said. It's right there on page one. It's the joke she says we've shared about me having two wives: the "before" and "after" version. That joke may have been made once, probably by Debbie, and I probably smiled and nodded or maybe even laughed out loud, but it's not true. You see that joke implies some kind of "once for all" magical change. A big decision that swept through everything. The miracle cure. The "before" and the completely transformed "after."

*Life does not work that way. I have not had two wives. I have not even had two different editions of the same wife. I have had just one. And everyday (and repeatedly through each day) she has been faced with the same decision, over and over. "How will I live my life today?" And **most** days she has made the choice to live in a way that glorifies God and honors me--not all days, and not at all times. The realization that her responsibility was to change herself and not to try to change me may have come as a great "eureka" moment, and the significant changing may have started from that day, but the decision to focus on changing herself is one she makes daily--and the changing is a daily process.*

And now, a story for you husbands.

A few years ago we were working with a couple who were preparing for ministry in their native land. He spoke English. She did not. One of his tasks was to read this book and translate it into their local language for use there. And as he read the book a sadly predictable thing happened. We began to receive word from him complaining about his wife. She was rebellious. She did not support him. She was not submitting to God. She was not honoring him. She needed to change. **She** needed to change.

OK guys. Confess it. If you've read this book or skimmed through it or even merely read the title you have probably, at least once, had the same thought. "My wife needs to change." Well guess what. I've got news for you. If you have thought that your wife needs to change, then **you** have missed the point--completely.

If I could write a companion book to my wife's **Changing Me**, a book written for men, the title of that book would be… **Changing Me**. That's right. For once in your life you have permission to say, with full conviction, "It's all about me!" Why? Because **you** are the **only** person **you** can change. And it is **your** behavior and attitude for which God will hold you accountable. Not your wife's.

In Colossians 3:19 God says, "Husbands, love your wives and do not be bitter toward them." He says that without any list of qualifications or pre-conditions. (And if you think **that** is hard, trying reading about poor old Hosea!)

I tell my wife that she is the single greatest manifestation of God's love for me that I know on this earth.* And that begs a question. If she is that to me, then what am I to her?

I think I'll go take out the garbage now.

*Does this bother your theology? Before God established the church, before He gave the indwelling of the Holy Spirit, before He sent His Redeemer, God gave Adam "a helper suitable for him." And it was very good.

I waited patiently for the Lord;
And He inclined to me,
And heard my cry.

He also brought me up out of a horrible pit,
Out of the miry clay,
And set my feet upon a rock,
And established my steps.

He has put a new song in my mouth—
Praise to our God;
Many will see it and fear,
And will trust in the Lord.

~ Psalm 40:1-3 ~

CPSIA information can be obtained at www.ICGtesting.com
Printed in the USA
LVOW01s1634150713

342969LV00007B/541/P